Mindset
Unlocked

Do What Others Can't, Won't, or Don't Do
for a Successful and Balanced Career and Life

CICI CASTELLI

Edited by Bianca Musetti and Giancarlo Musetti

BGLAND Publishing, Inc.

BGlandPublishing.com

ISBN: 979-8-9855603-0-5 (print)
ISBN: 979-8-9855603-1-2 (ebook)

Ordering Information:
Special discounts are available on quantity purchases by
corporations, associations, and others. For details, contact
BGlandpublishing@gmail.com or visit BGlandPublishing.com.

Papi,
thank you for believing in me.

CONTENTS

Part One

The Big Dos or Can Dos

Do What Others Can't,
Won't, or Don't Do

Finding success in the business world comes down to a formula that I have established and put into practice for myself over the years. Though we might all define success differently, I define it as the achievement of a happy, healthy, and financially comfortable or independent lifestyle in which I leave a legacy or impact other people's lives in a positive way. My success makes me feel energized every day when I wake up and grateful at the end of each day to have been able to make a difference in my life and in the lives of others. That is why I have decided it's finally time to share my secret to success with you. But first, I will have to take a few steps back...

I wish I could say I was born successful. However, even though I feel grateful for the healthy and happy family I was born into, I believe it was the decisions I made throughout my life—which took me out of my comfort zone and helped me to evolve into a better version of myself—that impacted my future and the trajectory that led to my success. I have seen great achievements and successes in the lives of people I have coached and mentored over my career. I have developed some principles on my own and some I have learned from others who I admire and see as extremely successful in both their business and personal lives.

What I have learned throughout this journey is that to win more business when working as a consultant, or to stand out as an employee, leader, or entrepreneur—and what I firmly believe is critical in succeeding in life—you must **unlock your mindset and do the things that others can't, won't, or don't do**. This means that I have used a specific set of tactics that no doubt began as business instincts and perfected them as behaviors, strategies, and tools to help me set myself and my teams apart while giving me a competitive advantage over others.

These practices also focus on and apply to more than just career success. Maybe that sounds counterintuitive, but when you sacrifice your personal happiness, wellbeing, and quality time with your family in order to gain success in your career, you might find yourself standing alone and falling short of your desired goals. Ultimately, if you don't create a comprehensive balance by nurturing your personal life and your business life, it will hinder your ability to achieve your career goals.

Learning to do what others can't, won't, or don't do has allowed me to climb multiple corporate ladders and spread these same methods to my teams, which has made a noticeable difference in my life, personally and professionally, and in the lives of my network and coworkers. It is time for you to reach for the life and career success you've always wanted!

"This is my wisdom for you: in order to succeed in every area of your life, you have to start doing what other people can't, won't, or don't do."

What I offer you in this book is a roadmap to developing your ability to do what others can't, won't, or don't do. I will show you how to extend that mindset to your team, and how to achieve success in your professional career while also maintaining a balance in your personal life. While each chapter topic in isolation could be thoroughly dissected in its own right, in this book I will share how I set out my formula for achieving team success and coaching others to succeed. Through the stories I share here with you, I will also demonstrate how my personal experiences have guided me toward knowing what needs to be done to set myself apart and reach all my goals. Even though some may not be new concepts to you, I will give you the tools you need to take the first steps toward a lifetime of success, personal achievement, and happiness.

Stephen R. Covey, who wrote *The 7 Habits of Highly Effective People*, has said, *"Most of us spend too much time on what is urgent and not enough time on what is important"* (Covey, 2003). He popularized the idea of the "Eisenhower Matrix," a quadrant comprised of the following categories: urgent and important; not urgent and important; urgent and not important; and not urgent and not important (Covey, 2020). Your life's destiny follows the quadrant where you spend the majority of your time. Successful people focus on the activities that are important and not just the ones that are urgent. You—and only you—can and will define what are the most important aspects of your life. Those that spend most of their time on what is urgent are average performers in their personal life and career.

Important and Urgent	Important but not Urgent
Urgent but not Important	**Not Urgent and Not Important**

Table 1.1 Urgency and Importance Quadrant

By filling out the quadrant, you'll see where most of your focus is, which will highlight where you may need to reallocate your time and effort. If you don't spend enough time on things that are important, for example, in order to make yourself successful you might need to rearrange. Similarly, if you only focus on what is urgent, you might miss out on personal happiness by not spending the time on what is personally important to you. Doing what others can't, won't, or don't do comes down to reorganizing the way you approach life, your mindset when it comes to what is both urgent and important, and understanding on a basic level what it is you really want out of your life and career.

Breaking free of the status quo is your ticket to the top! It is your pathway to high performance, success, and overall happiness. It is how you get noticed and stand apart from the average performers. As a manager, executive, or any leadership position, when you spread these tools to your subordinates, it creates a ripple effect of success that reflects positively on you. It also paves the way for them to become more efficient, more passionate about their work, more focused, and happier overall—leading to success for you and your whole team!

I first became interested in being a business coach when I realized I needed a coach myself. It began when an administrative assistant I worked with went to Human Resources (HR) and told them that I yelled at her in front of everyone in the office. This took place on a Monday, which doesn't seem important, but it turned out to be.

HR looked into the situation, but they couldn't find any witnesses that agreed I yelled at the assistant—they all said that I was just asking her for a status update regarding what she needed to have done. No one even said I raised my voice to her.

This experience was incredibly personal, and I feel vulnerable and somewhat exposed by sharing it with you here, but I want you to learn from my failures and shortcomings. I felt horrible for how the administrative assistant reacted, and for a long time it made me feel like I had a big "X" on my back, like my bosses had marked me out for some kind of disciplinary action, even though they hadn't. It felt like I was being watched closely for the next screw up. I felt like I was a failure.

I shared this experience with my kids as they were starting out in their careers too, as I wanted them to be aware of what they could get into. At the time, I was concerned that this one incident was denying me the promotion I'd been waiting a long time for—that it was impacting my professional future.

As upsetting as this event was, it unbolted and opened a new door for me in my career. I stayed rational and calm. I began to wonder whether there was something else that was preventing me from getting this promotion, so I decided to do something I'd never done before. I found the courage to go to HR to see if they could be an asset to me.

I spoke to them about how my bosses would promise me promotions, in writing, after my reviews, but would never deliver, while I continued to watch other people in my field be promoted. I told

HR that I'd been receiving five out of five ratings in my reviews and had an exemplary history with the company. It seemed like I just kept running into snags with promotions: my bosses would change, there was a general change in leadership, or they just couldn't create a position for me.

The HR department supported me and invested in me as an employee. This is when they recommended me and paired me to work with a coach. I started learning how to open up to a stranger and began to trust that person with my personal stories. I shared information about my bosses, my team, the office, and all kinds of career-related stories and experiences.

Ultimately, having a coach taught me to value myself as a high-performance employee, and having that accountability inspired me to consistently strive to be the best version of myself each and every day. My coach showed me what was missing from my own methods that I would need to master in order to succeed. A large part of what she taught me was how to achieve the right balance between my work and personal life. With her guidance, I was able to discover new mechanisms to successfully accomplish my goals, to acknowledge new and different perspectives that allow me to work with my team and other individuals the best way I could, and to accomplish personal and career-focused breakthroughs.

For example, the administrative assistant who had reported me to HR had needed me to be more personal with her. She wanted me to start Monday mornings asking about her family and her weekend rather than jumping right into work. I learned that by connecting with the other people in my office on a more personal level, we would all be able to work more effectively together, which would improve the office environment overall. I came to realize that taking the time to engage with my coworkers on a personal level about their weekends wasn't wasting time or company resources but rather strengthening our bonds and trust in each other so we could work more productively toward the same company mission. The bottom line in the breakthrough I made with the administrative assistant was that connection is as important as accomplished tasks.

Starting Monday mornings with a to-do list for my team, a set of problems that need to be solved, or a new project that needs planning is valuing a company more than the people who make a company successful. Therefore, when you put people first and you invest in forming deeper connections with your coworkers or your team, you are demonstrating that they come first. Although there is a fine line between personal life and work life, the habit of checking in with your team every day and getting to know them on a personal level will encourage them to work harder and value the work that needs to get done and will create a healthier work environment.

My experience with the administrative assistant was uncomfortable at the time but also valuable, as it helped me realize what was missing from my career path and encouraged me to seek the help I needed to become a better leader, and a better person, for overall success in my career and personal life.

I decided I wanted to pass on to you what I learned from my coach, because it has been so vitally important to my success. I believe everyone can benefit from such guidance, just like I did.

So, this is my wisdom for you: In order to succeed in every area of your life, you have to start doing what other people can't, won't, or don't do. I have coached many individuals that have shown rapid improvement and achieved great things by following my model. Don't settle for average when you can reach the full heights of your success!

All these stories or momentos are personal experiences that marked my life and my career and I would like to share them with you. I have changed the names of the companies and people in the stories to keep their privacy and confidentiality. Even though this is my personal professional memoir, I also hope it functions as a practical guide to help you, the reader, reach your professional goals.

My challenge for you is to read through this book, follow the reflection exercises, and answer the questions I pose. You'll be amazed to see what differences they make!

Plan for Longer Than a Day

S o many people live by the mantra of living one day at a time. It is true that we can choose to approach life this way, but what successful people do to reach their goals and continue to grow and succeed is plan for longer than just a day. The plan is what makes all the difference in the world when it comes down to organization, productivity, consistency, and efficiency. Colin Powell said in Oren Harari's, *The Leadership Secrets of Colin Powell*, "There are no secrets to success. It is the result of preparation, hard work, and learning from failure." He was right!

Think about when you have an exciting event coming up and you want to make sure everyone is on board with the time you're meeting, the location of the venue, the dress code, the duration of your stay, and what the plans might be after the event. For a second, let's visualize planning a beach day with a few friends and family members. We can all attest that coordinating and planning is essential, right? You must set off neither too early nor too late; the beach you pick should have enough parking—and you have to take into account if parking is free or not and check that everyone can afford to pay parking. You must also remember the snacks, water, umbrella, towels, sunscreen, tanning oil, volleyball, an extra set of clothes, and chairs.

Even though there are dozens of little details that go into planning a simple beach day, we can agree it does not take more than 10 to 20 minutes maximum to plan everything and get everyone on the same page. So, what if we plan each and every day with the same stringency with which we plan a beach day? You just take the last 20 minutes of your day to figure out all the details for the next day.

A few of those details can look like this: What time am I waking up? When am I planning to exercise? What am I eating for breakfast? When am I doing my laundry? Am I going to practice gratitude and write down three things I am grateful for in the morning or before I go to bed? What business meetings do I have on my calendar, and do I have everything prepared and ready to go? Who do I have personal meetings with?

Taking things day by day may work for some people but planning ahead of time differentiates average people from successful people.

I found that it isn't just important to plan for your career and your day-to-day activities. It is important to also make plans and set goals in other aspects of your life—hobbies, personal relationships, projects, and even mundane chores. I learned early in the game that successful people regularly book in their calendar time to review their goals, priorities, and roadmaps.

When and Why to Plan

What I do, that most people can't, won't, or don't do for themselves, is set time aside weekly, monthly, and annually to plan. I make daily plans, weekly plans, monthly plans, and even yearly plans. Some of you may think, "Oh no, that's too many checklists and will take up tons of time that I could spend doing all the things I need to do" (Tracy, n.d.). As Brian Tracy has said, "The rule is that each minute spent on planning saves ten minutes of execution." Therefore, spending 10–12 minutes of planning can save 100–120 minutes of your day. It is important to focus on the areas that move the needle forward, and not just on where you're busy in the here and now. When taking action your mind should be exploring these questions: "Where do I want to be one year from now? And five years from now?"

When I make a plan for myself, either short or long term, I also think of what I need to do in order to see that plan succeed. It is easier to picture and implement by planning the day-to-day and week-to-week tasks that are narrow and don't take up a lot of time or effort. Longer-term goals require more thinking and may be conditioned on smaller steps that need to be taken before they can be achieved. So, try to break them down into smaller chunks that you can act on, and set up some deadlines or dates to keep yourself on track to achieve them.

When you look at a long-term goal within a business context and the various steps needed to reach it, you'll also want to draw up a timeline for completing those steps. Each date in the timeline should initiate a positive or negative action if it is met. You do not want to be super busy and fail to meet any of your targets, so ask yourself and your team members if they can feasibly meet these dates and if achieving the results of those actions takes you further to meeting your goals. If it doesn't, ask yourself, "Is this activity really needed?"

Then stick these steps on a wall with sticky notes, write them on a wall calendar or on a whiteboard in your office space, or use an app so that you can make sure you reach your goal as planned. Even if the activities you list are small and feel insignificant, every achievement is meaningful, big and small, and they all create a snowball effect that will help you to succeed.

Unless you work on a construction project, in a software development team, in a well-structured organization run by a project management office, or in a team with published schedules, you will find that consistent communication with your team regarding goals and actions will become motivation to keep going. Moreover, having a full calendar removes all concerns of, "What should I do next?" or the doubts of, "What else do I need to get done or have I missed?"

These are the kinds of questions that lead to worry and anxiety, which should be avoided at all cost. A good plan removes doubts and is instrumental in building much needed consistency, momentum, and discipline. Whether it is a team activity or a personal action, when I wake up in the morning, I don't have to think, "Should I go to the gym today?" If it is in my calendar, it gets done. If it isn't there, then it simply doesn't get done.

One of the biggest mistakes that I have made over the course of implementing this habit in both my personal life and professional career is forgetting that it is all about consistency. Planning for 30 minutes intensely one day and not planning for the next four days after that is not as effective as taking 10 minutes each day to plan out the next. The habit of planning daily goals is very important.

Have short-term and long-term goals for your career, but also for hobbies, vacations, romantic relationships, friendships, family, your home, etc. Planning becomes more interesting and exciting because it allows you to look ahead when you schedule the fun times that you want to have in your relationships and social life as well as what you want from your career.

You can define for yourself how soon or how far away a short-term or long-term goal is. These goals can look different for everyone depending on the area of your life that you are making these goals for. For example, a short-term goal in the workplace may look like a daily task that you set for yourself to accomplish every single day, whereas in your personal life, your short-term goal might be buying a house in the next two years.

Here's another example: One person's long-term goal may be losing 20 pounds in one year whereas another person's long-term goal may be starting a family in five to eight years. The bottom line is that you have the flexibility to define the time frame for your short-term and long-term goals. And if you find yourself struggling with this, I recommend seeking a one-on-one coach or life counselor that specializes in assisting others with the planning, organization, and clarity. When you make a plan and follow certain steps and actions, it takes away uncertainty. Equally, lack of planning leads to distraction, over-thinking, and wasting time when it comes to "What comes next?" All of which can be stressful, overwhelming, and counterproductive.

In the context of a work environment, without having a plan, a team can be left floundering. No plan to follow and no objectives to achieve leads to confusion, an inefficient method of assigning work tasks, lack of focus, and an improperly handled workload. As an executive or manager, devising an action plan gives those reporting to you a clear path and direction to take. It also makes it easier to organize the work from start to finish, and to assign tasks within that project.

I once experienced witnessing a project team that was planning to execute a major renovation of a data center. The project was 10 years overdue and required a very detailed project plan and lots of work. The original project manager that was hired didn't have a concrete and detailed plan for the renovation, and several issues began to spiral up. I was asked to jump in as the project manager at the last minute to correct the mistakes that had been made due to the lack of a good plan.

There were a lot of problems, like the wrong parts being ordered, which no one had noticed until the old parts were unplugged and the new ones needed to be plugged in. At one point, my team literally had to go out into the dumpster and retrieve the old power cords. We cut the prongs off the old cords and put the old prongs on the new cords to keep the electronics up and running.

Every hour that the system was down, millions of dollars were lost in revenue. We were on the clock! If the original project manager had had a solid plan with buy-in and approval from the actual technical team that was going to implement it, if he'd dotted his I's and crossed his T's—meaning if they paid greater attention to detail—many of the problems we encountered would have been avoided. With proper planning and risk assessment, the fallout could have been managed without diving into the dumpster in the middle of the night!

The Importance of Revision

Another part of planning I do but that I have found many people can't, won't, or don't do is reviewing and revising my plans. Many people think that once they have a plan, they have to follow through with it, so they don't review or revise. Others will get caught in the trap of not wanting to let go of a plan or goal, even if it no longer serves them. They can't get out of that mindset and they can't move on!

When I set time aside weekly, monthly, and annually to make my plans, I also analyze, review, and revise those plans. I ask myself, "Are there certain goals that have changed, and do I need to adjust the steps and timelines? Are there goals that have been achieved and can be checked off?" Most importantly, "Are there goals that no longer align with what I want in that aspect of my life (like work, hobbies, relationships, etc.)?" And, "When thinking about my career and my team do I need to adjust my goals, actions, and deadlines?"

My daughter is 22 years old, and, although I may be a little biased, she is one of the most ambitious people I know of that age. She started a business in 2020 when she was in her last year of college and COVID-19 had just started. She wanted to be able to make an extra stream of income and became very passionate about continuing this business for the long term even when she finished college and it was time to start her career.

As an entrepreneur, she was so committed that even when it got hard, even when things would go south, even when the business was not growing as quickly as she wanted it to, she kept going—she stayed consistent. However, when she graduated from college and started her career, her priorities began to change and the goals that she made the previous year looked a lot different from the goals she started forming as a graduate. She was scared to tell me that she did not want to continue with her business for fear that I would perceive her decision as a failure. She had the wrong mindset and that is where I told her, "Quitting and understanding when to change direction to get what you want in life are two very different things."

Letting go of the plans that no longer serve your best interests or the path you are on is just as important as having the plan in the first place. Your focus needs to be on the end result and final achievement, not just on the plan. You don't want to get stuck in the mindset of needing to follow through with your predetermined plan if that goal no longer resonates with you, makes you happier, or provides you satisfaction or gratification in your journey to succeed.

Your focus may shift over a month, a year, five years. Review and, if warranted, revise your plan to align with changes in your focus so you don't get stuck doing something that you ultimately no longer desire. In his book, *Essentialism: The Disciplined Pursuit of Less*, Greg McKeown explains how everyone should make quarterly personal objectives to define the most important objects in their lives for the next three months (McKeown, 2014).

There is nothing less motivating than trying to achieve a goal that no longer fits into your life. On the flip side, checking off a goal that has been desired and is now completed is vastly encouraging, rewarding, and uplifting—like scoring the winning goal! And if you feel you are not aligned, then apply "another set of cognitive skills that might matter more: the ability to rethink and unlearn," as Adam Grant suggests in his book, *Think Again* (Grant, 2021). Rethink and let go of the views that are not serving you right now and be open to other people's opinions and teachings, which may help you to position yourself more strongly professionally or serve you better at a particular time in your life.

Revision of your plans is also helpful because you might be able to eliminate a few steps. For example, you might be able to shorten a timeline or add more steps and extend a timeline, both of which reduce stress in the long run. Planning is all about taking the pressure off yourself and your team and getting organized.

Planning can help you see where change should happen in your life and reviewing and revising your plans regularly can also show you how much you have developed and grown. It is a good way to track your own, or your team's, progress over long and short periods of time. That kind of roadmap is an incredibly helpful tool for getting you and your team where you want and need to be.

Revision of plans in a professional context can highlight, throughout the course of a project, where certain tasks might need to be reassigned, for example if one group is working faster than another. Maybe it looks like the initial timetable won't be met and revising the plan can help bring it back on track. Or perhaps the team is working faster than you thought and reviewing your plan refocuses your team's goals and timelines so they align with the business's overall goals. Revising plans provides opportunities to reorganize and re-prioritize what the team should work on, which keeps them engaged and provides you the valuable feedback needed to manage the project.

Getting Your Team Involved

As an executive or manager, you should implement these practices for yourself and also encourage your team and coworkers to look at their own plans. You want to start small, perhaps with a daily to-do list. Before the end of each workday or at night when you are winding down, look at your list and see what was accomplished and what wasn't. Make a conscious effort to focus on those things that weren't accomplished the previous day by adding them at the top of the new list for the next day, unless they are not important, in which case you can remove them from the list.

Your ultimate goal is to form new and improved habits that will become part of your routine. Everything in life changes and improves over time and you should always be thinking, "How can I make myself better or make this easier for myself?" Forming habits takes repetition; some say 21 days of repetition (Selk, 2013). One of the biggest mental blocks people tell themselves is that, "This is too hard," instead of asking themselves, "Am I being consistent or disciplined enough to see the results I want to see?"

When you start small, it is much easier to convince yourself that what you are doing is easy. You need to eliminate negative behavior and negative thinking entirely. Having the mindset of "I can't do this" will make it true. If you adjust and unlock your mindset to "I can do this," or "this is easy," it will *become* easier. I'm not saying that everything you choose to do is going to be easy but applying positive thinking and behavior will provide you with a path to follow to accomplish what you need to accomplish and remove the obstacles that are simply thoughts in your head preventing you from reaching your goals.

Don't keep these secrets to yourself: lead by example with your team members. Once your daily to-do list habit feels comfortable and natural, expand to weekly, then monthly, and then yearly lists. Make them simple and visual so that you can easily check or cross mark once you are done. Talk to your team members about how to make plans and break them down into a more organized schedule with manageable and actionable tasks. When your team hears your excitement and passion about the benefits of planning, it will inspire them to do the same.

For your team's plan, you should familiarize yourself with a calendar tool. There are so many technology-based tools out there and they change so often that I suggest you do some research and find one that is most suited to your environment. Some of the most popular scheduling tools are Google Calendar, Outlook, among others. Alternatively, display your plan on a wall calendar in the office where anyone on the team can see it, or track it in Smartsheet, especially if you and your team work remotely.

Not only does a visual aid help to keep everyone on task, but it encourages your team members to come to you with questions and update you on how the work is progressing. An in-office visual aid is also a good way to keep them accountable with each other and might even get them to think of how they can use similar planning tactics in their own personal lives.

If possible, try to get all your team members a desktop calendar or a packet of colored sticky notes to encourage them to use planning techniques in their own workspace for their workload. Extend praise and appreciation as further encouragement whenever you see them utilizing those tools. When people are supported and noticed for their actions and habits, it reinforces those good actions and habits.

You can also use a planning template, such as Table 2.1, as print-outs or electronic documents. Pass them around and think of incentives for your team members to fill in the information, such as recognition in a staff meeting or getting some vendors to sponsor gift cards and giving some out to the best planners, etc.

Start small, be a role model, encourage others to follow with passion and praise, and use visual representations that are easy for everyone to utilize. These tips will help you form a planning habit for yourself and your team and encourage your team to plan for themselves too. You should also foster an "open door policy" with your team so they feel comfortable coming to you with questions or concerns about projects, their workload, and the team's plan. Open communication will lead to clarity, effectiveness, and efficiency.

How to Plan

When you move beyond the "small" phase of planning, it can get a little more complicated, and this is exactly why visual representations are good. When you hit a certain point in planning, it becomes difficult to keep the details straight in your head. For example, as part of a long-term plan I might think, "What new skills in my personal development do I want to achieve by next year?"

Don't force yourself into an established scheduling routine. Everyone has different strengths and weaknesses, and you should use the method that jives with you best. If you are visually inclined, a wall calendar, sticky notes, or a whiteboard are probably preferable. If you are technologically minded, an app, Excel, Smartsheet, or a planning program might meet your needs better. If you travel a lot, having a planner book that fits in your bag could be the most useful method for you.

I start simple with my planning, dividing a piece of paper, section of my wall, or a document on the computer into four sections—the four quarters of the year. In my fourth quarter, I write down the desired goal for that year under specific categories like career, health, spirituality, etc. I then divide each quarter into three months, those three months into four weeks, and each of the four weeks into seven days.

Q1											
Jan				**Feb**				**March**			
Week 1	Week 2	Week 3	Week 4	Week 1	Week 2	Week 3	Week 4	Week 1	Week 2	Week 3	Week 4
Mon	Mon	Mon	Mon	Mon	Mon	Mon	Mon	Mon	Mon	Mon	Mon
Tues	Tues	Tues	Tues	Tues	Tues	Tues	Tues	Tues	Tues	Tues	Tues
Wed	Wed	Wed	Wed	Wed	Wed	Wed	Wed	Wed	Wed	Wed	Wed
Thurs	Thurs	Thurs	Thurs	Thurs	Thurs	Thurs	Thurs	Thurs	Thurs	Thurs	Thurs
Fri	Fri	Fri	Fri	Fri	Fri	Fri	Fri	Fri	Fri	Fri	Fri
Sat	Sat	Sat	Sat	Sat	Sat	Sat	Sat	Sat	Sat	Sat	Sat
Sun	Sun	Sun	Sun	Sun	Sun	Sun	Sun	Sun	Sun	Sun	Sun

Table 2.1 Quarterly Planning Template

Encourage your team to use a tool like Table 2.1 for their long-term planning. You can fill in the details right in an electronic document, print it out and hang it on a wall, or put it on your desk and fill it out by hand. If you use sticky notes, you can reuse the template over and over again. The pages could also be filed in a binder or planner to carry with you. By filling out four of these tables, you'll have your whole year planned!

Here is an example of a personal goal. In 2021, I decided I wanted to write a book. My Q4 goal was to have the writing of the book finished. Now, there are two ways to plan once you have your goal. You can start at the beginning and write down everything you have to do in order to accomplish your goal starting with Step 1. This is commonly referred to by project managers as "from the bottom up."

For some of my personal projects, I have at times found this method both overwhelming and distracting. However, it has worked effectively when I want to empower a team to come up with the date when their projects will be accomplished. The way I like to plan most of my personal projects or goals is to work backward. I give myself a goal and a completion date as a target, and then I fill in the steps backward until I reach the current calendar day. This has made me more efficient in accomplishing my goals. It also pushes me or forces me to achieve things faster than if I do not dictate a date to myself as a target completion date.

I've had people tell me before that rather than investing time in planning, they'd rather just act. As Brian Tracy said, "Your ability to set goals and to make plans for their accomplishment is the master skill of success." That seems good in theory, but it is harder to hold yourself accountable when you don't have a designated plan. Psychology professor Dr. Gail Matthews did a study on goal setting and discovered that you become 42% more likely to succeed in your goals and dreams when you just write them down! (Morrissey, 2017).

Digital apps or programs can be particularly helpful in planning because with some of them you can save a scheduling template and just fill it in as needed rather than building a new one every year. Some planners come with templates that can be easily filled in too. Then again, maybe you want the freedom to design your own planning and scheduling aid rather than using a pre-built template.

With practice, I have perfected a habit of coming up with a list of steps I must take to achieve my goals, and then I break those steps down further. I might ask myself, "What do I need to do in the next six months to reach my goal?" Then I'll break it down again and ask myself, "What do I have to do in the next three months to hit my six-month milestone?" With each milestone, I think, "What do I need to do to get there in the allotted amount of time?" Then I come up with smaller milestones and steps to fill in the shorter time span.

If your goal is to lose 10 pounds in the next six months, you need to break that down into mini goals that are going to help you achieve your overall goal. Your mini goals may look like going to the gym three times a week, implementing intermediate fasting five days of the week, drinking a gallon of water a day, and only eating sugars and carbs in moderation. By doing this, your mind is no longer focused on your six-month goal because you are more focused on the mini goals that are going to get you there. You now know "WHAT" you want to do and have mapped out "HOW" you are going to do it.

Sometimes you might forget certain steps as you are progressing—that is the benefit of reviewing and revising. Going back to my example, if I revised my third week of working on my overall goal and noticed that drinking a gallon of water a day was definitely helping me lose weight, but I realized that intermediate fasting was not working for me, I would revise my mini goals and redirect my approach in order to reach my end goal.

Over the years I have learned to keep a holistic view on what is important in an organization or for a particular team. When things arise unexpectedly, which they often do, I lead my team to continue their focus on what is important, which is planned out and scheduled. I focus on moving the needle forward with a balance between what is important and what is urgent overall, each and every day.

PUTTING IT INTO PRACTICE

KEY TAKEAWAYS:

- Plan longer than just a day.
- Set time aside weekly, monthly, and annually to plan.
- Plan short- and long-term goals.
- Regularly review and revise your plan to keep it relevant to your goals.

REFLECTION:

1. What do you or your team need to do in the next six months to reach your goals?
2. Think of what project you or your team need to start in the next 90 days.
3. Remember to add a calendar entry every week to "review and revise" your plans.
4. Remember: "If it is not there (in your plan), it does not get done." Is there anything missing from your plan that you need to add in?
5. Come up with a list of what you or your team are doing that does not move the needle forward, and then eliminate those things!

CHAPTER 3

Take Risks

To some, the word "risk" comes with negative connotations, and to others it suggests excitement and endless possibilities. I have noticed it can even be the kind of word that instinctively makes people feel nervous and promotes anxiety primarily due to the unknown consequences. In other words, risk is uncomfortable. However, true and measurable success is conditioned on some level of risk and most will admit that risk is necessary to succeed and grow. No company ever got off the ground and no entrepreneur or corporate executive has ever reached the top without taking risks, some minor, some major. In fact, taking risks is paramount to growth, change, achievement, and success.

"I attribute my success in life to taking risks and doing what most people in my position couldn't, wouldn't, or didn't do."

I studied risk management as part of my master's degree from Boston University. But let me tell you, it doesn't take a master's degree to learn how to take risks and manage the results. Some of our simplest daily activities in life involve some type of risk. Most individuals who are considered achievers, high performers, innovative, diverse, or "cutting edge" have considered risk in pursuit of greatness and pushed through those risks.

Identifying, analyzing, and planning in spite of those risks set them apart from the average and made them successful. It is easy to say that these people got lucky, but it is far more likely that they had the courage and utilized the tools of risk assessment, risk-taking, and risk management to give themselves an advantage over people that wouldn't or didn't follow the same model.

I attribute my success in life to doing what most people in my position couldn't, wouldn't, or didn't do. I had to become comfortable with being uncomfortable, having courage, taking risks, and assessing the potential benefits and fallout. I had to prepare so that I could minimize as much as I could and still reap the rewards. Yes, I am bold!

In the year 2000—during the dot-com days—I decided to move to Silicon Valley. I was working at director level in a hospital in Boston, but I remember thinking that I was so young and would not be able to climb the ladder any higher than director level in the medical field because I did not have a medical degree. I was driven to grow but felt limited in my options. After weighing different opportunities, I began to realize that I was better off shifting my entire focus to a new up and coming industry and starting from scratch in an area that had opportunities for growth.

Back then I remember reading in the newspapers that there were more jobs in the technology industry in California than there were people. I knew the risk in changing fields and careers, but I wanted more out of life and saw this path as a risk that would pay off in a major way. I took a leap and gave one month's notice; I packed up the house in Boston, grabbed my six-month- and two-year-old babies, and moved to Northern California to begin the process of finding a new job. I could not believe that I was moving across the country with two babies and no job, which I knew was a major risk, but I was confident in myself and believed that a job in technology would benefit me in the future and would provide me with the growth and personal development I wanted.

Benefits of Taking Risks

Most people believe that making the decision to change careers is risky. It probably carries greater risk when you choose to leave your existing job in order to make the career change, as you are not even sure about what level of success you'll be able to achieve in the new career. Questions bouncing around in my head were: "How am I going to climb that new corporate ladder?" "What type of new role can I secure?" "Will I like working in the new environment?" and, "Can I endure starting from the bottom, potentially making less money than I was, and working my way up again?"

I identified those risks and concluded that these massive moves were worth it to me for myself and my family's future. These are the types of things that I had to identify, analyze, and endure to make a successful career change. It is extremely important to look at every area and prepare yourself mentally and emotionally for what could go wrong, but also for what could go right. Ultimately, your analysis should cover the positives and the negatives of every action. Your focus needs to be on what you would do if something went wrong. This is the definition and the art of risk management.

I've learned that there are two ways that executives and team leaders approach and handle risk. On the one side, there are those who will willingly take the risk and accept both the positive and negative outcomes, whichever arise. Then there are leaders and managers who are "risk averse." Their tolerance to risk is lower and they come across as folks that take a good deal of time to present more of the negative outcomes to everyone around them. And then, of course, you have those that are not only risk averse but who also won't personally want to own the liability or take responsibility if anything bad happens.

Risk assessment is a multi-layered analysis of evaluating what the outcome will be. It means balancing what the positive benefits can and will be versus what the negative outcomes could be. Then it is a careful consideration into whether or not the gain of the positives outweighs what could be lost by the negatives. Sometimes the ends don't justify the means, at which point it is appropriate to be cautious. Throughout the process of risk assessment, we should continually expect to identify different levels of risk.

However, being overly cautious limits growth and may lead to stagnation. Risk-taking brings with it change and action. When I was 17 years old, living in Caracas, Venezuela, I made the decision that I wanted more out of life. I was hungry to get out of my country and move to the United States so that I could learn English, become the best version of myself, and leave an impact on the world. My strict Hispanic mom and Italian dad were strongly against the idea of me, a single young woman—or girl in their eyes—ever moving to a different country, because Venezuela was our home.

So, I did what any 17-year-old, ambitious (rebellious) teenager would do: I packed my suitcases and told my parents I was just going to the States for one year as an exchange student. But in my mind, I knew I was never going back. I couldn't ask for their permission to stay because I knew they would never let me go, especially since I did not know English at all. That is when I knew I had a strong enough personality to face my fears and take the risk I felt like I needed to take to be where I am today.

Back then I knew nothing about risk assessments or risk management, but I did have the courage to take the associated risks. In my mind, the risk of coming to the United States from Venezuela outweighed the risk of staying there. Today I can look back and know that thanks to the steps I took in the 80s, I am able to provide my family with a safe haven in the United States, especially with the current political and economic situation in Venezuela that has spiraled into a crisis and has made living there so difficult.

Risk Management Plans

Risks can be adaptive and can lead to positive outcomes. When assessing risk, I believe it is far more beneficial to focus on the positives—will it save me time and money, enhance my reputation, and provide substantial benefits? Based on my experience of managing critical technology projects, I have learned that when planning we must also anticipate and have a contingency plan for any of the potential issues that may materialize from the risks.

Part of risk assessment is risk management—which is a whole book in itself, but here you'll find the basics. Proper risk management entails developing a plan to counteract and overcome negative outcomes. You need to be honest and communicate transparently with everyone affected by your decisions within your team and the broader organization. With a detailed, thorough risk management plan and great communication or expectation management, any fallout can usually be managed in a way that lessens the negative impact. As a result, even if the desired outcome wasn't achieved, thanks to your risk management plan you can still maintain trust with those that have been impacted.

Taking risks should be factored into your short- and long-term plans. Since there is a good deal of risk involved in change, you should be sure to carry out a full risk assessment for all your professional and personal goals.

I take a lot of risks. From an outside perspective, it could seem reckless, but I feel that, professionally, I have perhaps been more noticeable than other project managers because I am willing to take risks when others can't, won't, or don't. I also analyze each risk and make an informed decision rather than letting the fear of negativity or backfire from the fallout limit my actions. With a proper risk assessment, good team communication, and expectation management, you will be able to open more doors, do more than others, and achieve what others don't at your same level.

If you fall into the "risk-averse" category, you should fully assess the risk benefits before taking any action. You may not have the know-how or desire to come up with a risk management plan but by putting risk-taking, risk assessment, and risk management together you can take your work and your impact on your team and within your company to a much higher level.

Make a name for yourself as the "risk-taker," but also as the "risk manager," and you'll stand apart from anyone who is over-cautious or "risk averse." Encourage your team and provide them with the tools to build their own risk assessment, risk-taking, and risk management plans. These methods can be applied to more than just work-related risks.

Two years ago, my current employer asked me to move to our China office in Shanghai and live there for two years as an expat. I was to represent our team as a leader in the digital technology field. I was expected to break my apartment lease, sell my car, and leave most of my belongings in a storage facility for the time I'd be away. In addition to that, I had to decide whether I was okay taking the risk of being so far from my boyfriend at the time and family in the US for that long. Of course, this decision required many changes and a lot of risk-taking: There were many things I would have to learn about Chinese culture and its language, and I'd never worked in China before, so I did not know what to expect.

However, taking this risk ultimately provided me with knowledge, realization, experiences, and the greatest value from my life and career. I got the hang of saying "Zaoshang hao," to my coworkers every morning and practicing Tai Chi at the park every Sunday. I was finally growing in a new part of the world, immersed in a new culture with new customs and new professional responsibilities. Until my experience was completely interrupted and impacted by the COVID-19 pandemic of 2020.

Coincidentally, early in 2020, I had to fly from China to Miami for a three-day departmental meeting, right around Chinese New Year. Because of COVID-19, I was stuck in the US indefinitely and could not return to China for my assignment.

The pandemic is an example of an unforeseen risk factor that impacted my plans. I endured many challenges when I got stuck in the US during that time, such as not having any of my belongings with me (I had only come for a three-day meeting after all). I lived in 11 different hotels and had to deal with all the uncertainty that affected countless others during the pandemic.

I kept waiting for my office to give me the green light to go back to China to pick up where I had left off. But as time passed, the COVID-19 situation worsened, and I never got the okay. I ended up having to stay in Miami and having to wait nine months for my things to sail into the US on a cargo ship. However, to this date, and despite the downsides, I still know and believe that taking the risk of moving to China, living the life of an expat, and experiencing what the opportunity provided me outweighed *not* taking the risk.

"Risks can be adaptive."

Assessing Risk

Leaders have the responsibility to encourage their teams to push forward and take risks. They can do this by encouraging them to respectfully challenge the status quo while feeling they are in a safe environment where creativity is promoted and praised. This allows new and innovative ways or ideas to emerge. From there, your team will realize that some risk-taking may be required to execute those new ideas and ultimately reap the rewards and benefits.

If you are the team leader, it will likely fall on you to be the voice, wisdom, and impetus behind risk management. However, by getting your entire team involved in the risk management framework or process and procedure, you create a healthy and collaborative culture that will continue to grow as they learn to take more risks. According to a 2008 Project Management Institute conference paper entitled, "Risk Analysis and Management," having a team-structured risk management framework will help ensure earlier and more effective communication on any project issues that arise, a stronger team-building tool, and conscious and focused risk assessment and risk management.

The same conference paper identifies key concepts of risk management including: continuous risk identification, evaluating the risk, mitigating the risk and defining contingency measures, monitoring and control, and measuring risk identification efficiency (Lavanya and Malarvizhi, 2008).

"You should get your entire team involved in the risk management framework or process and procedure, making it intrinsic to team culture."

Each project your team works on—and each risk taken in your and your team's personal lives—should undergo a simple risk analysis at the very least. This should include: a list of possible risk sources and categories; the probability or likelihood of negative impact; a well-developed action plan to reduce risk; a contingency plan of what you would do if a risk arose; and the risk threshold or the value that measures if you will accept the risk or not.

Project:

Risk Categories/ Sources	Probability for Positive Impact	Probability for Negative Impact	Steps to Reduce Risk	Contingency Plan

Continued Risk Identification	Risk Evaluation	Monitoring/ Control	Risk Threshold

Table 3.1 Risk Assessment and Management Template

The above table outlines how risks should be assessed and handled from the very beginning, as well as what continued measures should be taken throughout the duration of the project. When working with your team, you should consider having a large visual representation of what the risks look like for the project or a virtual document that everyone on the team can edit and review. Knowing the potential risk and having a management plan adds levels of comfort and takes away uncertainty as your team works through the project.

Since continued risk identification and evaluation is an important part of working through any project, giving your team members the ability to update those sections in a collaborative way that the rest of the team can see and benefit from—and add their input and insights to—will make them more effective and able to grow their skills within risk assessment and management. This all leads to everyone involved being more comfortable with risk-taking!

It should be obvious to you who in your team is a risk-taker and who has a "risk-averse" personality. A way to encourage a productive risk-taker mentality is to make it part of the culture and the company's core values, and ultimately to reward, or praise, the teams or members that take responsible risks.

Google "fosters an environment where employees are praised for taking risks," (Schneider, 2018), back in 2006 TOMS launched the one-for-one program, where they would give away one pair of shoes for every one purchased. In 2019, they did away with this program and instead are putting a share of their profits into a fund. This is actually an example of an original risk gone bad, but they pivoted according to *Forbes* magazine, (Hessekiel, 2021). There are many other great examples of companies that make risk-taking part of their culture.

PUTTING IT INTO PRACTICE

KEY TAKEAWAYS:

- Risks can be adaptive and lead to positive outcomes, self-development, and growth.
- Leaders have the responsibility to encourage their teams to push forward, take risks, and feel they are in a safe environment.
- Use a risk management plan for each project and risk you take.

REFLECTION:

1. What are the risks in the project that you need to start in the next 90 days (from Chapter 2)?
   - What are the potential positive and negative outcomes that could result from starting or not starting the project you mentioned in Chapter 2?
2. Let's do a quick risk-analysis exercise:
   Step 1: Identify any risk, hazard, or impact in your personal life (for example: Deciding between staying in your current job (X) or taking a new job offer (Y); having a career change; starting a new project, etc.).
   Step 2: Figure out the impact of your action on anyone else involved (for example: New job Y offers 10% more money than current job X).
   Step 3: Assess how severe the risks may be and what actions you may be able to take, and then note them on the risk assessment chart (for example: New job Y would require many more hours, which means that your kids would need to be in aftercare for longer).
   Step 4: Review the risk assessment and decide if it is worth taking the risk or not (for example: The risk assessment may potentially show that the aftercare cost increase may be larger than the actual salary increase and that therefore new job opportunity may not be worth the risk). Of course this is a simple example, as there may be other reasons to take the new job even though it may not offer a higher pay incentive. For instance, it may offer a better career growth path.

CHAPTER 4

Embrace Challenge

How do you approach challenges? Maybe you see them with mild indifference, acknowledging that a challenge has presented itself but not taking any action to pursue or embrace it. Perhaps you run terrified and find a place to bury your head in the sand. Then there are the people like me, the ones who welcome a challenge with open arms and can't wait to dive into it!

Why is it that a lot of people prefer to avoid or dismiss challenges? The word challenge implies difficulty and can feel heavy. For some people, rising to meet the challenge could be more trouble than it is worth. To this date, when I observe how others in my field of work face challenges, I see another perfect opportunity to set myself apart as someone who charges straight into battle, embracing whatever challenges I encounter when others can't, won't, or don't.

Consider this: In a work environment, if you are the type of person who avoids challenges but your coworker is always jumping at the chance to try something new, who do you think will be noticed for opportunities that lead to advancement? The business world likes people who can solve problems and challenges as they can venture outside their comfort zone.

I have worked with and observed many people that always think and voice how difficult things are and never seem to reach a resolution to a problem. If their mindset were to unlock and shift from, "This is too challenging for me," to "How can I resolve this?" or "Let me resolve this," the challenges would end up stimulating growth in a way that doesn't happen within the confines of a regular routine.

The Importance of Accepting Challenges

When you don't accept or face challenges, a few things can happen. First, you limit yourself. You put yourself in a windowless room, too afraid to open the door and see what is on the other side. There is no room for growth, no opportunity to see or experience new things. Where you are is where you'll always be.

Being in the midst of a challenge is where you are going to mess up the most, but I believe that the most beautiful thing about making mistakes is that you are actively learning and growing. Think about this: If you go to your nine-to-five every day and are not trying new and different things and do not challenge yourself to be the best in your office each day, you are providing the bare minimum value to your company and to yourself, and no one wants that. This applies to both professional challenges and to challenges in your personal life.

Second, you are more likely to be passed over for promotion or advancement. Anyone who wants to progress in their career is going to have to show that they have the fortitude to cultivate leadership skills while facing challenges or tasks that are seen as challenging. Promotions and leadership roles tend to come with more responsibility and challenges. Hence the more you accept challenges, the more appealing you will be to your superiors. In your personal life, if you are known by friends and family as someone who doesn't like to take on challenges, you could be excluded from some adventurous group activities because the expectation is that you'll say "No."

Finally, when you don't rise to challenges regularly, if an opportunity comes along that is something you want to do, you are more likely to be passed over for someone who has accepted challenges in the past. You need to establish your "street cred" as someone who can, will, and does accept challenges in many areas before you'll be able to claim the opportunities that really strike your fancy.

How to Work Through Challenges

Challenges can present themselves in your personal life as well. It could come in the form of new experiences, a difficult argument or conflict with your partner or spouse, being a parent, learning to bake bread for the first time, etc. One of the ways I work through challenges is through trial and error. You have to find what works right and what works well for you, for the situation, and for anyone else involved.

If you've ever cooked to a recipe, like making a pie crust from scratch or baking a loaf of bread, you know you could follow the recipe to the letter and still find the end result isn't exactly what you wanted. The same is true with a lot of other challenges in life. If you gave up after the first attempt, though, you'd never know what it was like to achieve success.

Think of great inventors like Thomas Edison or Nikola Tesla. They have provided humanity with great technological advancements like the light bulb and the Tesla coil, which have each brought new advancements and comfort to modern-day life. It took trial and error and determination to get it right. The first time Edison managed to illuminate a light bulb, it only stayed lit for a few hours, so the inventor experimented with different filaments to get a longer-lasting bulb (The Franklin Institute, n.d.).

Embracing challenges means that you may need to step out of your comfort zone, take on a new and/or difficult task, and persevere until you reach the desired outcome—even if that means trying several different angles or approaches and learning how to deal with your feelings on the way. When you then succeed at a challenge, not only does it help you stand out, but it is also a huge plus in the win column! Giving up or accepting loss too soon is a major impediment to success.

I began to take on all kinds of challenges in my personal life and career, because I saw that other people couldn't, wouldn't, or didn't. Even as a young project manager, I would witness my peers voicing all the reasons why a project could not be done. Whether it was out of fear of the difficulty involved or of damaging their reputation, lack of knowledge, indifference, or whatever the reason, I knew I didn't want to settle for "average" or "easy" because that would prevent me from getting where I wanted to be. Different from my peers, my approach became to figure out solutions, think around the problem, and bring up ways that a project could be done while also stating potential negative impacts and managing management's expectations, instead of just listing all the reasons why it couldn't. This is where I got my "Cici gets shit done" reputation.

With each challenge accepted and overcome, I learned more about what I was doing—or attempting to do. I learned new skills to deal with events across many different situations, but more importantly, I learned more about myself. I identified my own strengths, developed resilience, mastered my emotions, cultivated leadership skills, and built character. It is no coincidence that the people we admire most are those that have embraced and overcome challenges in their life.

"Anyone who wants to progress in their career is going to have to show that they have the fortitude to cultivate leadership skills while facing obstacles or tasks that are seen as challenging."

After coming to Cambridge, MA as an exchange student in my senior year in high school, I attended Northeastern University in Boston, where I chose to study Deaf Studies and American Sign Language (ASL) Interpreting, because I wanted to become an interpreter for the Deaf. As an immigrant from Venezuela, English was already my second language. I was told repeatedly that there was no way I would succeed as an interpreter with ASL as my third language when I had not yet mastered English. There was one professor in particular who even failed me in many tests I took while mentioning I would never be "fluent"—talk about feeling that some people are out to get you.

Seeing this expectation of failure as a challenge, I decided there was no way I was going to give up! I proved that professor wrong when I graduated from the Interpreting program. I even found employment as an interpreter in a community agency for the Deaf in Boston. I worked for many years as a successful interpreter with both the Deaf and Latin communities. I worked in courthouses, and in the 90s I even established interpreter services departments in two hospitals in the Boston area! Let's just say this was one of my biggest professional milestones in the States.

Changing Your Attitude

Having always been told I was going to fail, it would have been easier to give up or switch to a different field of study. I realized, while living as an immigrant, that if I wanted to make it in the US, I needed to learn and do what an American could not, would not, or did not do. And back in the early 90s there were only six certified Sign Language interpreters who were also fluent in Spanish. So, even though ASL was not uncommon, what was uncommon was being able to translate a conversation from English to American Sign Language and then to Spanish or vice versa. I wanted to do something different, something that no one else could do. And I wasn't willing to sacrifice that goal based on someone else's negative opinion of me and my ability to prosper in this country.

Not all challenges you face come with another person telling you that you won't succeed. More likely, it is the voice inside your head telling you that you can't do it. If you always think that you can't, then you make it true. You've got to change your attitude and unlock and control your mindset to thinking, "I *can* do this," or "I *will* do this."

Even if you don't know the outcomes of a challenge you accept, by taking it on, you open up new doors, new opportunities, and new growth. This attitude helped me to approach challenges with a positive mindset while helping me learn more effective management and how to handle and welcome change as I moved through my life.

Helen Keller said, "Every struggle is a victory. [...] It teaches us that although the world is full of suffering, it is also full of overcoming it." Now, I charge straight into battle, and you should too. Say "Yes" when others say "No!"

Helen Keller was born deaf and blind and was unable to communicate with anyone for the majority of her childhood. The woman who taught her sign language, Anne Sullivan, had to change her approach to teaching so that Helen could understand the signs without being able to see them. She would sign words and letters into Helen Keller's hand so she could feel the shape and understand what was being communicated to her. Despite all the challenges she faced, Helen Keller always kept going, and thanks to her perseverance and ambition she became a famous writer and a role model on how to face life's challenges (History.com, 2019).

Leading Your Team to Embrace Challenges

I see challenges as problems, and problems need solutions. When your team faces a challenge, the first step is to identify and understand the problem that needs to be solved. And since I have learned by working with engineers that the best way to solve a problem is to break it down to the smallest possible components, I have been able to implement this method with my teams. Smaller problems or problems broken down into chunks are easier to solve. Show your team that all challenges are just problems that need solving, and they will be able to conquer them in both their work and personal lives.

If you want to encourage your team to be open to challenges you must be open-minded, foster clear communication, trust them, and allow them the proper time to get acquainted with the challenge or project. Give your team the opportunity to learn and understand the actual problem at hand—build their confidence to take on new challenges and support them all the way.

Problem-solving is a team effort, and if you create a work culture for your team where you are open to receiving solution suggestions, then your team will actively participate in the problem-solving. You can ask your team to come up with risk assessments when they have found a solution they believe in. This helps them to understand the viability of their solutions and compare their success potential to other solutions that are presented. By letting them take the initiative, you allow them to build independence and resilience as a team.

You want to be able to have more than one option when tackling a problem. I've come across many problems that take more than one attempt to solve (which I elaborate on further in Chapter 5). So, if your team comes to you with every little problem they encounter, you have created the habit of making them believe that finding a solution is only *your* job. However, when you lay down the expectations with your team at the outset and encourage them to come to you with problems and at least two to three feasible solutions, then you are leading your team to embrace challenges and solve them independently. This always increases your success rate and with time it will become a team habit. They will never show up with a problem without several options as solutions.

When I work with my team through challenges, I make myself their sounding board. I am open to receiving their ideas, and I support them through the process. As a leader I am not there to solve their problems, but I let them become problem-solvers themselves and encourage them to implement their ideas, which in turn builds their confidence to take on challenges and be comfortable presenting solutions. This is your role as executive, leader, or team manager.

I also believe that all solutions should be heard and presented. This might sound obvious, but you should not tear down, criticize, or belittle your team when they present a solution, even if it is not the best solution in the world. Rather, approach it from a risk assessment and risk management perspective so they can see what solutions are prioritized over others. Make it an objective process so no feelings are hurt.

"Problem-solving is a team effort."

Combining risk assessment with taking up challenges and problem-solving will take you and your team far in both your professional and personal lives. It is a matter of being open-minded to difficult situations and approaching them instead as puzzles to be solved.

PUTTING IT INTO PRACTICE

KEY TAKEAWAYS:

- Accepting challenges opens doors of opportunity.
- Trial and error are a fundamental aspect of working through challenges.
- Unlock your mindset and attitude to overcoming challenges and struggles.
- Problem-solving is a team effort. Let everyone in your team participate in brainstorming the solutions. Encourage everyone to present a different solution and never criticize a suggestion.

REFLECTION:

1. What is your top personal or career challenge today?
2. When you think through the problem and break it down into manageable chunks, what are the top items to accomplish? Think of what the different problems are and which smaller problem you can get started with first.
3. Think of two different ways to solve the problem.
4. Execute a risk assessment (refer to Take Risks, Chapter 3).
5. Now go after embracing the challenge!

CHAPTER 5

Be Willing to Start Again

Going back to the "trial and error" concept from the previous chapter, which I know does not sit well with many of my engineering friends, I believe there is an aspect of success that is often overlooked and that is a willingness to start again. One of the greatest tools I have used for my own success has been my willingness to start over. At 17, I left home and moved to a new country by myself. I had to completely start over in building my home, my education, making new friends, and learning to live in a foreign country without any loved ones or family support.

"When you think of starting again, think, 'What will I learn from this? How will I grow? What great opportunities are waiting for me or what opportunities can I create on the way?'"

Twice since coming to the US, I relocated my home (once across country and once across the world). When I moved from Boston to California, it was in search of a career that I could grow in. I went from being a director in a hospital to starting in one of the lowest roles as a project administrator in a technology firm because I wanted to get into technology. I had to start all over in my career, had to work my way back to the top, but it was a field I was more interested in and one in which I could continue to develop. I made this career change all with the mindset of starting again in search of greater opportunities.

By beginning again on numerous occasions, I have been left with a treasure trove of diverse experiences, some of which I now pass on to you.

Starting over is something a lot of people can't, won't, or don't do. People get comfortable in a certain position or situation. Comfort may lead to being stuck, which then decreases the number of new opportunities that come your way. In short, by refusing to take the leap and start again, you close yourself off, either to opportunities that could help you advance or to realizing that what you had was the best and to appreciate it as such.

When you aren't willing to start over it is most likely because of fear, so growth and change come very slowly, if they come at all. You miss out on a lot of great opportunities that could otherwise set you on the right path to success. It could be that you do not start in a management position, but you need to start somewhere. Knowing when to start over builds character. Actively putting your plans into action is what is going to help you achieve your goals faster and help you to create the most resilient version of yourself.

What Does it Mean to Start Again?

The concept of "starting again" has been stigmatized as a setback. People assume they've failed if they need to start again or that it will take them longer to get to where they want to be. Truthfully, I've found that starting over is just the opposite! Every time I have had to start again, I've been able to fall back on my experiences and knowledge from previous attempts, and that has given me a clearer path to get where I want to be. Knowing that you have fallen before and have hit rock bottom gives you the feeling that nothing worse can happen. I am always willing to start again, if needed, if something fails. This mindset has allowed me to conquer any self-doubt and become fearless.

"One of the greatest tools I have used for my own success has been in my willingness to start over."

If you and your team are working on a project, and the team dynamic or the project's progress begins to sour, the entire project could become a massive flop. However, if you take a step back to look holistically at what went wrong, you can take your team back to the beginning and start over to reestablish a healthy team dynamic and then work toward success.

This is just like the story I told you about my daughter. Knowing when to take redirection is essential, just like knowing when to start from scratch is important. If you and your spouse or partner get into an argument, sometimes you both need to take a step back and then start the conversation over to figure out how to talk through your disagreement without it getting heated or intense. I think we have all been in a conversation where we may not have liked someone's tone, and we say, "Alright, let's try this again and start from the beginning."

Have you ever known anyone who is reluctant to leave an unhealthy relationship because they don't want to rebuild a relationship from the ground up again? Maybe you know someone who has never been promoted but won't leave their job because they don't want to drop back down to an entry-level position. Here is an example: I recently presented a job opportunity to someone who I knew has been unemployed for over a year due to the 2020–21 pandemic and who needed a job. When I asked if he was interested, he refused to even hear more information about the position simply because it was not at management level. He told me he was not prepared to start from scratch and preferred to continue being home unemployed!

There are many scenarios in your professional life and personal life that could benefit from you starting again.

I've listened to coworkers and friends talk about changing careers and what it would be like to be back on top in their new work environment. I rarely hear them talk about starting back in an entry-level position and working their way back to the top. I've stopped assuming that I will always be "on top," which has helped me feel passionate about the work I do, even if I have to start in a "lower" position than what I left. This has also made me realize it is not always about the job title because you do not need a title to lead. A title does not define you. With experience, you learn that a title may make you more money, but it does not make you the best leader. At the end of the day a great leader always holds the highest potential to grow individually and financially.

Being fearless and starting again is about implementing the lessons you've learned from your personal life, careers, and relationships to avoid making the same mistakes again as well as about progressing faster to achieve your own success. Choose what area in your life you think you could use a fresh start in and give it another try.

Encouraging Others

Being in a leadership role means that you are responsible for encouraging your team to explore their options, even if that means starting again. You can do this by creating a work culture that doesn't punish the team for failure and, most importantly, rewards them when they try new things.

Part of allowing your team to try new things and allowing them to fail is providing the leeway for them to discover what works and what doesn't work. That skill and practice is what will help them every time they choose to start again. Whenever your team encounters something that doesn't work, let them know it is the perfect opportunity for them to start over and try something new.

By promoting this kind of work culture, you remove your team's fear of making mistakes. This can help them take more risks and accept more challenges. You want to give your team the space to be "self-starters," allow them to work independently, and encourage them to try—even if the results aren't perfect. By building this type of mindset in your team, it will generate opportunities for them, and for you, and create a more autonomous work environment so you won't have to micromanage them—leading to efficiency and productivity.

"Being in a leadership role means that you are responsible for encouraging your team to explore their options, even if that means starting again."

Starting again isn't limited to your career or work-related projects. With the tools you give them and the fearless mindset you instill in them, each member of your team will have the confidence to start again where they need to in the rest of their lives too.

Embracing Change Positively

It's true, starting again can be scary, but it doesn't have to be. If you're confident in who you are, know what you want to achieve, and use the methods that other people in your position can't, won't, or don't do, you will find—just like I have—that starting over leads to opportunities! However, I know many of us may doubt ourselves so that confidence or courage comes from having a plan and being comfortable accepting challenges and taking risks. When you put it all together, starting again becomes a chance to make yourself better than before and gives you an opportunity to seek better things for yourself in all aspects of your life.

One of the fears that comes with starting over that I've heard from other people is that they don't want to go back "to square one," or they don't want to give up what they have for something less. I read a book several years back by Mark Sanborn entitled, *You*

Don't Need a Title to be a Leader: How Anyone, Anywhere, Can Make a Positive Difference. This book was such an inspiration that I passed it along to some of my team members and they also had a positive reaction to it.

What Sanborn tells us in his book is that you can still have the qualities of a leader even if you aren't in a leadership role or if your company has not given you the title (Sanborn, 2006). When you present those qualities in a work environment, it doesn't take long for others to notice, including your superiors. I used the message of Sanborn's book to encourage people I worked with to not be afraid to start over again and instead act as leaders. Because, in the big picture, it is about who you are, how you work, and what value you bring to the table.

I always say, if you want to be the CEO, you need to act like you are the CEO, especially the CEO you want to be. Just like if you want to be a leader, act like the leader you want to be. The difference between a title and a leader is that a title tells people who you are, but a leader shows the people they lead who they are capable of being. That is what is going to get you to the top!

When you are considering starting again, think, "What will I learn from this?" "How will I grow?" or "What great opportunities are waiting for me or what opportunities can I create on the way?" As a leader, when you support your team members in starting again, you show them that there are options to explore beyond what they expected and that makes room for exponential growth. It also increases their passion and motivation for day-to-day tasks and work because they know what else is out there for them.

If you are willing to start again, you are willing to move forward.

PUTTING IT INTO PRACTICE

KEY TAKEAWAYS:

- Be willing to start over. Starting again isn't the same as failing.
- Being a leader means encouraging your team members to start again when it is needed.
- When you start again, you have all your knowledge, expertise, and experiences to fall back on.

REFLECTION:

1. What area of your life needs a fresh start?
2. Is there a good opportunity in another company at a lower grade than your position today?
3. Is moving an option?
4. What are the pros and cons of starting that lower position or new relationship, going to a new company, moving to a new country or to a new department, or starting that new project?
5. What is the end goal of starting again?
6. What are my fears? How do I overcome them?
7. Who will be impacted by it? Who are my supporters?
8. What steps must I take to make it happen? Execute a risk assessment.

Let's do it!

CHAPTER 6

Never Assume You Are the Smartest in the Room

One of the things I learned when working as a consultant was to always surround myself with the best people to do a job or a project and to not assume I am the smartest person in the room. I have learned to put my ego aside and be humble, and I'm okay with being the first person to say, "I'm not an expert in this area." What other people can't, won't, or don't do is to be humble about how knowledgeable they are or hire and surround themselves with people better than them.

When building my teams, I would hire people with strengths that complemented my weaknesses. Rather than thinking I am the best because of my leadership role, I strive to surround myself with the most knowledgeable people I can find. I put people on my teams that I know I can leverage and learn from, with more varied backgrounds, experiences, and expertise. My team members complement each other and together we can tackle any circumstance thrown at us.

In the wise words of Steve Jobs: "It doesn't make sense to hire smart people and tell them what to do; we hire smart people so they can tell us what to do" (Schwantes, 2017). Having worked with many teams, I have noticed that people sometimes fear being outshined by their peers who may be better at doing a task or a presentation than they are. What other people can't, won't, or don't do is embrace others that can share expertise and knowledge.

If I don't know the answer to something or have the knowledge in a particular area, I encourage my team members to come forward if it is something they are familiar with. If that isn't an option, then I am always willing to work with my team to grind out a solution and get the answers.

Work Smarter, not Harder

To work smarter, I have developed habits and routines that are strong and efficient for myself as well as my team. I am not one that loves to have meetings for the sake of them, since I want to make sure my team and I have enough time to get the work done during working hours so that we do not have to take work home or extend the day. I don't want my team to miss an opportunity to have a good work–life balance.

Most days we start with a quick meeting to sync up. The meeting is in the team's calendar, so it is prioritized over other activities and is expected by everyone. These meetings are concise and provide alignment. We discuss our priorities for the day and the team can get clarity on conflicting priorities if in doubt. Also, in case anyone is depending on me or on anyone else for a decision, this discussion provides visibility into why someone is not accomplishing their tasks. People share what they have achieved and what they have completed. Ultimately, the entire team works as accountability partners.

Then, we schedule time for quick meetings throughout the day for when anyone needs clarification or follow-ups, so that the morning sync-up meeting continues to be a quick and upbeat discussion that sets the day for success. I have observed that this approach has kept my teams organized and in check and creates more pro-ductivity throughout the day.

One of my specialties is coming up with fresh ideas to save labor and effort by making my teams work more efficiently. Decreasing the overall company cost while maximizing efficiency and pro-ductivity is one way to work smarter. I have provided a valuable resource to companies this way in the past and knowing this gave me confidence—I felt inspired and was willing to do whatever else was necessary. So, always look out for ways you can reduce cost or leverage the resources at hand.

What other people can't, won't, or don't do is to look away from what benefits them and their team alone and consider what bene-fits the organization holistically from the point of view of resource utilization. By doing this myself, I developed an uncanny ability to figure out how to leverage skillsets that individuals had in different teams to the benefit of a project or a department.

For example, when I worked in telecommunications back during the dot-com era, one of the senior managers asked me to figure out, account for, and log what each person in engineering did. By working in Excel and using enterprise project management tools, I developed and mastered the skill to do this holistically for a research and development engineering organization of a few hundred engineering resources. All based on a holistic point of view and not on what would benefit only one person or one team. Fast forward to my current employment, having had over 10 roles within different teams, I have developed many relationships and the ability to identify the best people to assign to different projects based on my detailed knowledge of each individual's skillset across the business and who is best suited for a particular project or to work on a technical issue or challenge.

Having worked with so many individuals is a great privilege. Not only to have made many friends and expanded my professional network, but the exposure to so many people from different walks of life and cultures and with different skills has been eye-opening and a lesson in itself.

In addition, when building teams, I would ensure they are able to operate effectively without me without the fear that if they did so, I would become indispensable. I had to look for people that had strengths and knowledge to get the job done while I was able to move on to the next project or attend other priorities.

This was a huge growth opportunity for me, as I was able to work in a different area while simultaneously still setting up my team up for success if I was ever absent or unable to work with them directly. Sometimes life happens, and it gives great peace of mind to know your team can handle their responsibilities without you looking over their shoulder—that is working smarter!

When I went to work in the China office, my team remained in the US. At the time, we were rolling out our new release management processes for digital mobile apps in the organization. There was a 12-hour difference, so I could not attend any process meetings with the engineering or product teams. But I trusted my team, and they were successful independently from me. This is a great example of growth and trust in a team and shows how we were able to work smarter instead of having me awake all hours of the night and dialing in from China. They accomplished it, they prepared their risk assessment, and they executed it successfully.

Working smarter and holistically means taking a step back to view the entire company as a whole. Sometimes, I will put myself in my boss's shoes, or the CEO's shoes, or in the shoes of my highest leader. I'll look at how all the teams contribute differently—I don't want to favor one or pick one out of the rest, or else the entire company loses productivity. From that viewpoint, I think about what benefits and serves the entire organization, not just any one team or individual, but based on the priorities of the organization. I learned, from working in organizations that are projectized, that when teams are all divided up according to project, sometimes it can become like working in silos and at times there is no one looking out for the organization as a whole.

Narrowing this mindset back to your team, you don't want to always be siding with one team member or only thinking of your own success and advancement. You should consider what will benefit the whole team the most and put that into practice. I once had an experience with a leader that showed me what *not* to do. This particular person had different areas within his team, each with a different manager and he always encouraged competition with and between them.

Although healthy competition may be acceptable in a sales organization, his team members were always working against each other, which generated many conflicts between the teams and ultimately became counterproductive for the company as a whole. It would have been more efficient to look at the entire portfolio for the efficiency of the organization and developing strong relationships and trust among his leaders and not just the benefit or success of each individual team.

Working smart extends to being efficient in your personal life too. Do you have chores piling up? House renovations that need doing? A vacation or event to plan? By working smartly and with a holistic view of all your work and personal activities, you can decrease your stress, increase your productivity, and have plenty of time for yourself too!

There are other ways working smart comes into play in your personal life. Consider a long-term romantic relationship, for example. If you aren't great with money management or with time management, look into the skills of your significant other and see how you can complement each other's skills. Think of the people in your life—your partner, friends, and relatives—as your "life team." What is it you can contribute to the relationship and how does that offset what they can contribute?

Humility in the Workplace

Working smart isn't about being smart or always being right. If you can admit when you are wrong or don't have the answers, your team will respect you for your honesty and your humility. It builds trust with your team and gives them a chance to step up and provide new information. When the whole team gets involved, it creates a "work smart" culture.

Last year, I was approached by my leaders to implement a critical project for the industry to return to service after we had been at a halt for months during the COVID-19 pandemic. The project was to implement probably one of the most innovative technologies—that had not even been tested yet—across the world with all the global logistic protocols that entailed.

When looking to see if this was doable, many people brought up all the difficult risks and challenges we would have to overcome. My approach was not to be egocentric, suggesting that I knew more than everyone else. My role was to be involved from the beginning of the project with the attitude of a leader that perhaps does not have the answers but who works together with the team to grind a solution until we are successful. When I surround myself with the best people, I can listen to and learn from the subject matter experts. Remember that everyone on your team will have knowledge and experiences that can differ from other people. Let them know that and make them feel valued for their contributions. You will see that when you encourage them to fall back on what they know for the benefit of the whole team, they build trust and work efficiently together.

Encourage your team to be resourceful and observant. Teach them to be facilitators and to be of service to their team and to the organization.

"As a leader, when building teams, I would hire and look for members who had strengths that complemented my weaknesses."

How does humility lead to success? Well, I learned that when I don't constantly showcase my skillset, I become an observer and that creates an opportunity for learning, growth, and change. You can learn a lot from the people around you collaborating as a team if you just listen and observe and give others an opportunity to show you what they can do.

When it comes to embracing humility, Gandhi was an example. He said, "The seeker after truth should be humbler than the dust" (Gandhi, 1993).

Executive Presence

Executive presence is not about getting things done; it means being the leader that others want to follow by inspiring confidence and trust in your peers, having integrity and poise, and being able to command a room. It means showing that you are reliable and capable while also inspiring confidence in your own leaders that you have the potential for greater achievements.

Sylvia Ann Hewlett explains in her book *Executive Presence: The Missing Link Between Merit and Success* that the three factors for success are poise, confidence, and authenticity. She discusses how an effective leader should carry on a behavior of being in charge, how a leader should act, how they should communicate, and how they should look.

This is an important concept in working smarter without thinking you are the smartest. You want to project this confidence in yourself so that your team wants to follow you and be loyal to you as their leader. That same executive presence is what your bosses will see when they consider you for promotions and advancements in responsibility.

While having executive presence is based more on your behavior, it still qualifies as a technique for working smarter. I have deliberately included the concept of executive presence near the section on humility as a reminder that you can be a confident and effective leader without losing that humility.

Having executive presence goes hand-in-hand with working smarter, but not at the expense of thinking you are the smartest.

PUTTING IT INTO PRACTICE

KEY TAKEAWAYS:

- Hire team members that complement your weaknesses.
- Bring humility into the workplace.
- Have executive presence, integrity, and poise, which will inspire confidence in your peers.
- Work smart without thinking you are the smartest person in the room.

REFLECTION:

1. What are new habits and routines you can build for you and/ or your team?
2. Think of the skillset that each individual team member brings to the table. What are the areas of expertise of each that you trust and how can they complement each other?
3. Take an inventory of their skills.
4. Show that you trust that person by delegating something to them and letting them contribute.
5. How do you think your team sees you?
6. How do you behave with your team during stressful situations?

CHAPTER 7

Raising the Bar Through Change

A friend of mine told me he thinks I am always "hungry," always seeking ways to improve myself and be a better version of myself. As human beings, we are constantly changing, and growth comes from change. Change can happen naturally, but you can also welcome, encourage, and embrace change in yourself and in others for more targeted improvement and success.

Remember in Chapter 2 when we talked about making plans and revising them? One of the things that I do when I revise my plans is think about how I can make them better, how I can improve myself through planning and goal revision. Based on my experience, I've run into a lot of people that can't, won't, or don't consistently raise their own bar. They become satisfied with the minimum or staying in their comfort zone and never try to excel beyond that.

I have a friend who wanted to lose weight, so he got an exercise machine and began working out for 10 minutes a day. Once he hit the 10-minute mark daily, he never went beyond that, so his muscle tone and endurance stopped progressing beyond what he reached with those 10-minute workouts. And even though this exercise was progress and helped him emotionally, 10-minute daily workouts aren't rigorous enough to consistently lose the weight he wanted to lose, build muscle, or improve endurance. But he decided that he didn't want to challenge himself. This may work for him and his emotional wellbeing. I suggest you ask yourself what you need or want in order to better yourself.

You might think that you are exactly where you want to be, and that might be true, for the time being. However, everything is constantly in motion and changing, so you don't want to get too comfortable, or restrict your self-development, by telling yourself you never need to set higher expectations.

In the past few years, the world has experienced a global pandemic, an economic crisis, high unemployment rates, and restrictions on travel and other daily activities. If that has taught us anything, it is that life never stops, and change can happen in an instant. Did everyone just conform with the huge changes that this pandemic caused?

No! Governments and medical teams around the world pushed themselves to develop treatments and vaccinations, restaurants adapted their dining services so they could stay in business, companies set up remote work from home for their employees. And in the travel and hospitality industry we have worked day and night to ensure a successful return to business by planning and replanning to address the constant changes in protocols while reinventing the industry to continue to provide amazing vacations.

These were steps that were taken to "raise the bar" on what life had thrown at us and make our living situations, work life, and financial situations better than what they had become.

On a personal level, you can set standards and expectations for yourself that make you feel proud. Reach for yours in daily, monthly, and yearly goals that give you fulfillment and help you achieve your own success. There is always room for improvement, even if you are in a great place. For two months, I had a daily goal of reaching between 10,000 and 11,000 steps every day during my daily walk. Once I hit that goal, I didn't plateau and let my step count remain the same, I thought, "Can I comfortably increase this to 12,000 steps a day, or should I play it safe and only go up to 11,500 steps a day?"

Reaching a goal doesn't mean there isn't something beyond that to strive for. Raising the bar means that when you reach a goal, you set yourself new ones that take you to the next level. This is how you grow, change, develop, and create the life and career for yourself that you want and deserve.

I love where I am in life. I'm proud of my accomplishments, and I thrive on the work that I do. And I'm never going to stop striving for more, for better. How about you?

Expectations

Life and work expectations are different from plans and goals. There is some overlap, but a plan or goal is your tactic, your strategy for striving to get something or accomplish something. Expectations are what you think you deserve or what you anticipate happening or who you anticipate becoming. You can't fulfill your expectations without plans or goals.

For example, when I wanted to become a business and project management consultant, I planned to take the Project Management Professional (PMP) exam to add this certification to my credentials. My expectation was to earn this certificate in a few months. Hence, I had to come up with a plan to achieve that.

Expectations are limitless, or they should be. Hence the phrase, "The sky's the limit!" What limits a lot of people is thinking that they aren't good enough or smart enough, that they don't deserve anything better. To me that is all a lie. Everyone deserves the best, and anyone can get it for themselves.

I believe that you should never reach a point in your life where you can't grow, improve, or develop personally and professionally. Not only should you always be positive about this, but this should be your goal. You just need to have the right mindset, believe that you can do it and believe that you are good enough to have it.

I have a close friend who always compliments my time management and planning skills when he brings up how much his business is in need of new systems and processes. However, when I make suggestions on steps he could take and the discipline required, he immediately retorts that of course I can do that because I have a project management background and he does not. Well, I did not have the same background all my life. I have adapted, studied, and learned how to implement new methods along the way with discipline, consistency, and a mindset of being open to change.

I have failed many times, allowing myself to learn from my mistakes. However, my expectations of myself have always been that with a good plan, patience, and consistency I am able to improve. The fact that I failed English as a second language in Venezuela wasn't going to prevent me from speaking English, becoming a simultaneous interpreter, and now writing a book. Just because I was an immigrant and I slept on a mattress on the floor in a place with no heating system, or the fact that I did not own a refrigerator and used to place my milk right outside a window in the winter when I first lived on my own in Boston, wasn't going to prevent me from putting myself through school and earning enough money to have the comfortable lifestyle I have today.

Your past does not dictate your future, so do not let negative thoughts control your mind, telling you that because you were once poor you cannot become rich, or that because you did not get an education you cannot succeed. Think of where you want to go, set your mindset, and develop your plan to get you there!

The Domino Effect

Increasing your own standards can have a domino effect on other areas of your life. I consistently analyze the standards in my sleep habits, eating and exercise patterns, relationships, in my role as a mother, in my career, my living situation, my family dynamics, etc. There isn't an area in your life that is too small to be improved upon. Now, this does not mean I sit around analyzing my life every day, either.

This domino effect happens when you make the decision to raise the bar in one area of your life and you find that you need to raise the bar across multiple aspects of your life to remain consistent. Start with something small, like improving your sleep habits by sleeping an extra hour or having a bedtime routine or look into your nutritional habits. You'll notice quickly how the dominos begin to fall and you have room to grow all over the place! Think of an athlete preparing for the Olympics. She not only has to train, but also get enough sleep, have the proper nutrition, get the right medical care, massage therapist, etc. It works the same way.

As a leader in your workplace, this domino effect not only impacts your own life, but it also spreads to the people around you, especially those on your team. When you raise the bar for yourself at work, it also raises the bar for your team. It is important to offer support to your team when these expectations change so they have the proper time to adjust.

Over time, they too will be striving for greater things, and the domino effect will ripple out into their personal lives too. A lot of team leaders can't, won't, or don't encourage their teams to seek higher expectations for themselves. When they get a good team together, they want to keep it that way. Be the kind of leader who promotes higher expectations, not just in their team's work performance, but also in what each team member wants from themselves.

In 2015, while working in the travel and hospitality industry, I took a special assignment that required me to travel for about two months in the Middle East and Asia. My two children, who were teenagers at the time, came with me as I am a single mom. I thought that would be the only solution at the time. It was close to the end of the school year, so I pulled my children out early. My daughter, who was a sophomore, and my son—even though he missed his high school graduation—certainly didn't mind!

I thought there would be nothing more valuable than taking them across the world, not only to learn about my projects and how technology was being deployed, but more importantly, to experience new countries, cultures, languages, foods, customs, and traditions. (However, seven years later I can say that the domino effect bit me in the ass as my daughter has become the bougiest person I know, booking trips left and right, but I mean hey! At least we know she works hard, so she can generate enough money to live and to afford her own trips now.)

My assignment was to oversee a technical team that had to successfully accomplish over 20 critical projects before we arrived in Shanghai. As we went across the world, we were planning to be in some amazing cities where I assume we would take the opportunity to sightsee and explore new cultures. As we were preparing to be in one of the first cities, I asked the team what landmarks they wanted to see so that I could efficiently plan our day.

It was my first time leading this type of international project and I was completely blown away by their response. The team looked at me with so much confusion on their faces, wondering why on Earth I was asking them what they wanted to see in each country. You see, although they had worked for several years in the industry, including traveling this way internationally, many of them had never previously taken work breaks to include in their trips visiting different places.

They had never had a team leader that encouraged them to have a break while in the many countries. So, even though we were going to amazing cities they all assumed they would be working all the time and of course somewhat sad for missing out. I was shocked and worried. I promised my kids to see all these countries, not to just come to see me work!

So, at our next meeting I explained that I was implementing some scheduled half day or time off for them. Even though this was a shock to some of my leaders, and many gave me a hard time for doing it, I stood up for the team and promised on behalf of my team we would still deliver our projects flawlessly. I trusted them and, of course, we delivered. In return, the team worked harder the days we were not going to go out sightseeing.

They worked longer hours and did whatever it took to be able to see Oman, Malaysia, Vietnam, India, and Singapore, among other places. To this date, I have coworkers who I worked with on that project that continue to ask for opportunities to work together again. My motto was, "Work hard, play hard." However, I simply saw it as a work–life balance, especially when you are in a work environment 24/7. What I did that others previously couldn't, wouldn't, or didn't do, was set new expectations for my team that they would have this work–life balance, despite being far away from home and the office.

That was the moment when the domino effect really played a part in the success of my project. Do you want a team to finish a project 10 times faster, efficiently, and successfully? Easy. Create a happy team! Through leading this project, I learned that giving back to my team made them more eager to work harder and feel recharged when they came back. Never again did this team skip a day of exploring the world when they had a chance.

After this project was successful, it actually opened new and unexpected career opportunities for me. I was eventually offered a new leadership role in this project management area of the company, a role that I held for a few years.

I share this with you because you can set yourself apart by being the manager that helps your team establish higher expectations in their careers and personal lives. If they have an interest in a different position, you could help by coaching them so they ultimately get to the position they want. You can practice for the interview with them, and you can leverage your contacts to help them. If they want to learn a new skill, you can provide them with resources to help them along.

Not only does this set you apart, but it builds deeper trusting relationships between you and your team. It creates a sense of security in the workplace, which leads to happier employees and more passionate workers. Helping people raise their own expectations also has a domino effect. Nobody should have to stay in a position if they want to do something else. So, help them grow!

Think about your current job and position. What could you do to improve that position without applying for a different one? What could make you more valuable or happier in your current role? Is there a new language you could learn, a technical or soft skill that you could improve on?

We are driven by growth and development—our lives and careers depend on it for advancement. I don't have the same expectations and standards that I was working toward five years ago because I brainstormed how to create a better version of myself and what more I could reach for to fulfill my personal and professional ambitions.

PUTTING IT INTO PRACTICE

KEY TAKEAWAYS:

- Increasing your own standards can have a positive domino effect on your life.
- Keep raising the bar for continued progress, change, and improvement.
- Don't settle for "good"—keep challenging yourself to be "great."
- Work and life expectations are different from your personal plans and goals.

REFLECTION:

1. Start with your professional position. Where do you want to go? What are you doing that is routine and too comfortable for you?
2. In what area do you see yourself growing?
3. How can you get there? Who can you work with or leverage?
4. In your personal life, how can you take your health and your physical activities to the next level by raising the bar?
5. Where else in your life can you reach for higher expectations? How do you see yourself raising the bar?

CHAPTER 8

Never Give Up

66 I 'd rather die than give up the fight," is a line from the song *White Flag* by Bishop Briggs. I've adapted that line for myself: I would rather fail than give up! I believe that resilience is a muscle that needs to be worked on or practiced every day in order to become stronger. Resilience and persistence are built by not giving up and not backing down. Don't be the person who looks back and thinks, "If I hadn't given up, I would have accomplished this..." When you are resilient and you persevere, success will come your way. Greater things will manifest for you.

Too many people I know can't, won't, or don't persevere. Instead, they give up when things take too long or get too difficult. They give up if they think they aren't good enough, or if it takes too much effort, or if they hear that something can't be done. We are surrounded by instances in everyday life where people didn't give up and were able to achieve great things. I have trained myself to think that the faster I fail, the faster I succeed.

At one point in time, electric cars were considered an impossible fantasy. Now major car brands are each coming out with their own line of electric cars from small sedans to pickup trucks! Success is reached when you stop listening to the cries of, "That can't be done," "Not now," or "You aren't qualified." What people can't, won't, or don't do is adopt the mindset of never giving up.

Resilience and Perseverance

Almost everything in life takes hard work, a certain amount of patience, and commitment. In both your personal and professional life, make the commitment to yourself that you will be happy, you will be successful, and that you will get what you want. Once that commitment is made, hold yourself accountable with perseverance and resilience to make it through all life's obstacles until you achieve that success.

If you and your partner or spouse get into a fight, do you both give up and end the relationship? Of course not! No one would ever have long-term relationships or get married if the first fight became the last. It takes work and commitment to solve those differences. The same applies in your professional life.

Having a plan is the first big step (refer to Chapter 2 for a refresher on planning). You'll still need the commitment to see it through and a mindset of not giving up if you want to achieve the goals that serve your desire for success and happiness. Writing something down on your to-do list increases the likelihood that it will get done, but you are still the power behind the machine. And if it is not on the to-do list, then don't do it, because it is probably a distraction!

By combining a "never give up" mentality with planning and being willing to start again, you have three incredibly powerful tools that will propel you forward to navigate challenges. As easy as it sounds, truly understanding the power of following through with your goals until you have accomplished them is one of the main factors that differentiates average performers from high performers.

Here is an example. When I was 17 years old, I came to the US as an exchange student. I came with the expectation that my biggest challenge was going to be learning English. I was placed with an American family in Cambridge, Massachusetts, and discovered after a few weeks of adapting to American life that the family was dysfunctional. The mother was a victim of domestic violence and the daughter tried to commit suicide three times while I was living there. Then she was placed in a mental institution, and I ended up having to take a bus for an hour after school to go to their family therapy sessions.

Even though I felt terrible and wanted to help her—and to this day I wish I could have kept in touch and been of help to her—I found it all very overwhelming. My plan had been to come to the US to learn English and the American culture. I had come alone, and my parents were not happy that I was here, so I couldn't tell them what was going on—I feared that they would get on the first flight to come and pick me up and return to Venezuela. So I continued with their family therapy and tried to support the girl until it got to the point where I needed to find a healthier environment to live in. I contacted the exchange student company and told them what was happening.

I really lucked out because I had made a strong connection at the time with a young woman named Heather, who became a friend. She extended a hand and her family allowed me to stay at her house for a month while the exchange student company found me a new host family.

Well, it could not have turned out better, as when the company found me a new home a month later and came to get me, Heather and her family decided I was a part of their family already, and I should not leave them to move anywhere. To this date, I consider her my American sister. I am grateful to have built the resilience to have gone through the various incidents in my assigned host home and despite that experience still chose to stay in the US with a new family. I was not about to give up or go back home, which would have been the easier way out of that situation.

Another example of where I had to draw on my resilience was in 2010. I was in a soccer field practicing with my daughter and she did a cartwheel. I remembered how I used to do gymnastics growing up, so I went ahead and did one myself. Believe it or not, I landed beautifully, but the following day when I woke up, I went to get out of bed, stood up, and immediately fell on the floor. I was unable to walk. A vertebra had come out place and blocked the nerves to my legs, and in addition, I'd herniated a few disks. I needed immediate surgery.

I was told there was a risk I wouldn't walk again or that it would take at least six months to recover. I was so devastated I was even unable to drive for three months and I took it upon myself to do some research and instead of doing physiotherapy once a day, I did it three times a day—in the mornings, at noon, and in the evenings—until I was able to walk well and had regained my strength a lot sooner than the doctors expected!

It is important to remember on your journey that achieving career and personal goals doesn't happen overnight. Success will come when you don't resign yourself or compromise your own beliefs. Greater things will happen with the right combination of resilience, perseverance, and a mindset of never giving up.

Empowering others to believe in themselves is an important part of leadership. I do this first and foremost by believing in myself and by having confidence in my own abilities. I show my team that I won't give up. I walk the walk for them, rather than just talking the talk. I do this in my personal relationships too because it increases my chances of success and happiness.

Too many times, I have seen people give up prematurely, thinking they can't do something. Later, they discover they could have overcome that hurdle, and because they gave up, they missed out on some great opportunities.

Do yourself a favor right now and make the commitment to yourself to remove the phrase, "I can't do this" from your lexicon. Tell yourself every day, **"I can do this!"** Tell your team every day, **"We can do this together!"**

The Upside to Failure

It seems to me like a lot of what leads to giving up is fear that we need to work too hard at achieving something, or simply fear of failure. If someone tells you that you can't do something, you might start to believe it too. Then you'll stop trying. I believe that there is value in all experiences when you persevere, even failure.

If you fail, you've still accomplished something. You've learned how *not* to do something. You've learned what *doesn't* work. Maybe your initial objective wasn't reached, but you have new experience and ideas that you didn't have before. That is an accomplishment. If you give up, you don't even get that—you just get stuck with a lot of thoughts of what might have been.

With the experience of failure, you can start again, like we discussed in Chapter 5. Only, the next time, you're that much closer to succeeding. Never giving up means that if you do fail, you won't walk away. You'll get back on the horse, flex your resilience muscles, and try again. Back in the 90s, I decided to start selling my translation services as a consultant (yes, selling is part of being human and working as a consultant requires you to win new clients, so selling your services is a must). I learned that for about every 10 rejections, I would get one new client. In my mind, the faster I got rejected 10 times, the faster I would get that new client. In other words, the faster I failed, the faster I would succeed. I couldn't take it personally that some people didn't want to hire me as a consultant.

A story of failure and resilience that was very impactful to my future was the fact that I failed English in high school in Venezuela. Just like in the US where you can take Spanish as a second language, I needed to pass English in my senior year to graduate but believe it or not, I failed. The funny part was that my goal was to learn English so I could come and live in the US to begin with!

It was a desire, a goal I had before coming to the States, so I didn't let not knowing enough English stop me from moving. I ended up coming as a teenaged exchange student only speaking level one broken English. In one year, I had mastered the language. I still have an accent, but not only did I learn English, but after only a couple of years I became a simultaneous trilingual interpreter and worked at various conferences in Boston.

The benefit of failing is that at least you are still moving forward, still progressing. You've gained new knowledge and experiences, and you will continue to grow. Giving up stops growth and limits you to being stuck in the same old place. That is why I say I would rather fail than give up. I'd rather keep moving and building new habits of consistency and discipline than think that I'm not good enough or that I can't do something I want for myself.

"If you fail, you've still accomplished something."

Accepting failure allows you to develop the critical skill of adaptation. If you fail, you have to adjust and adapt in order to correct what went wrong. Adaptation becomes an invaluable skill to use in all areas of your life. It can be especially crucial in your work environment as things are always changing. You don't need to fail in order to adapt, but failure is a catalyst for building that skill.

I always told my kids when they went to a job interview that they had nothing to lose. If you give it your all during an interview process and they call you back to let you know that they went with another candidate, you might feel that you failed since you did not get the job, but really it is still a win because you learned from it and you can examine what you can do differently next time.

If you can start to see failure as a learning opportunity, you can teach yourself to never give up due to fear of failure. When working with your team, if something goes wrong or doesn't work out as planned, emphasize to them what can be learned from that experience or how they can adapt to make the best of it.

Teaching critical adaptation and acceptance of failure will empower your team to use those skills in their own work and their own lives. Practicing will encourage them to grow their resilience and perseverance muscles, and they too will adopt the mantra of never giving up!

When you decide what you want in your career and in your personal life, don't just give up at the first curveball thrown your way. Make the commitment to yourself and your team that you will see it through to success. Be the person that can, will, and does persevere and never gives up!

PUTTING IT INTO PRACTICE

KEY TAKEAWAYS:

- The benefit of failing is that you are still making progress.
- Switch your mindset to: "I'd rather fail than give up because at least I've accomplished something."
- When you are resilient and persevere, greater opportunities come your way.
- Failure is the catalyst to building new skills.

REFLECTION:

1. Think of a couple of projects or actions you want to take on but are afraid of because you might not be successful right away.
2. Ask yourself: "What is the worst that can happen? Can I come up with ideas to fix what goes wrong, or will I be able to try again after I fail?"
3. How can you compensate for what can go wrong? Mitigate it? Prevent it? And if you try again, would you succeed?

CHAPTER 9

Be Consistent

Almost anyone can have one good meeting, come up with one good idea, or show excellence every now and then. What most people can't, won't, or don't do is manage to do this all the time. When you are consistently on your game, it illustrates something special, something valuable to both employees and employers alike. Ultimately, through your display of consistency, you build the reputation of someone who is reliable. When I mastered building this reputation for myself, people started calling me Cici, the one that "gets shit done."

Once you have proven that you are consistent, your leaders and coworkers no longer have to take an educated guess, or a gamble, on your potential or your ability. This sets you apart from everyone else around you. Having that reputation as the person who is consistently on their game and gets things done will open up a lot of doors and opportunities for you. It will also increase your value in any employment setting.

I think many of us feel that when we get a new job, we have to prove ourselves to our new bosses and peers. Well, what I am talking about here is really the opposite. When everyone already knows that they can count on you and your team because you are so consistent with your results, the feeling of having to prove yourself goes away.

It is because of your consistency that you become excellent at what you do. Being consistent ties right back in with the difference between settling for average and striving for success. In my opinion this is where the phrase, "Practice makes perfect" comes from. Building your own sense of self-worth is a major asset in personal and professional success—it will make you stand apart from your peers and give you an added boost to achieve your goals.

The Promise of Consistency When Working with Teams

Being consistent builds trust with your team because they know what to expect from you every day. It offers security and comfort and is a huge step toward fostering a positive work environment where your team will be more likely to relax and focus on their work, making them more productive and more efficient.

Inconsistency leads to uncertainty. When things are uncertain, it is human nature to go into an adrenaline-fueled fight-or-flight mode. If your team is stuck in survival mode because they never know what is coming, their work will suffer, as will their happiness and passion for the job. Part of your responsibility as a leader is to make the work environment healthy and consistent!

I once was asked to lead a $34 million project that had already had four leaders before me that had failed at delivering and implementing the project. Over $28 million had been spent and the project was considered a total failure, plus the team at the time was almost burned out. Even though there were things that went wrong under my watch, many of the team members told me after we had delivered the project successfully in only a few months that one of the most important characteristics that I had brought to the team was consistency.

Before I had come onto the project, the higher-level executives would come in every day and ask this team of about 100 people what they were working on. The team would give them an update and then the executive might have a change of priorities and ask them to work on something else, leaving the first project unfinished. This would happen at least once a day, if not more. Labor was constantly being redistributed, and nothing would ever be completed. When I took the position, I would meet with the executives directly and if they told me to move my team onto a new project, I wouldn't tell my team until after they had finished what they were currently doing.

So, I made sure that even though the higher-ups were inconsistent on their goals, I prevented them from telling my team what to do. I decreased the amount of change they were encountering daily. The team would start to work on something, and instead of being interrupted the next day with a change of plan because "so and so" said so, they were finally being guided to finish the initial task. I learned that the inconsistency of directions the team had been exposed to from their leaders was preventing them from focusing on the right thing, and on the right tasks, and therefore cut into productivity and efficiency.

Consistency is key in your duties, goals, vision, and leadership. Your superiors will trust you more with new responsibilities, knowing you'll consistently "get stuff done" and always be at the top of your game. This is a prime opportunity for you to lead your team by example, but also impress upon them the importance of consistency in their own work.

During performance reviews, discuss consistency as an avenue to greater opportunities and the benefits of it in the workplace. For example, there have been times when I'd rather have a consistent employee who isn't as technologically proficient as required, because through the consistent "get stuff done" mindset and a disciplined attitude to succeed, that knowledge will be gained. Through their consistent behavior I can gauge their work potential, and I trust that they will acquire the knowledge they need to succeed. Importantly, that employee will also continue to carry disciplined consistency through the ranks.

To Err Is Human

While consistency is important to success and removes variables, I think it is also worth pointing out that as humans, we all still make mistakes. Being able to admit to and own your mistakes will set you apart from your peers. I've noticed a lot of managers and leaders throughout the years that always try to find a way to cover their asses or find a scapegoat to preserve their own reputation or image. I opt to own my mistakes.

When you take responsibility for the errors you've made, this shows your team and your bosses that you are honest, humble, and willing to do what is needed to correct the mistake. When you make a mistake, think of it as an opportunity to develop an action plan to fix the problem—I'd recommend bringing this action plan with you to your boss when you confront the mistake. It shows another level of initiative and commitment to your work.

Those extra steps in handling mistakes will make a huge difference in how you are seen by your team and your employers. If you don't have a consistent resolution approach for handling mistakes, it can become an issue, for example, if you expect someone else, like a boss or employer, to take control and fix things for you. You want to manage your own mistakes and the mistakes of your team to demonstrate that you are a great asset to your organization.

The Great Benefits of Consistency

We live in probably the most fast-paced, least predictable of times and in a generation that has become more innovative and quicker to judge than ever before. This has made me understand the importance of providing a consistent style of leadership that contains comfort and certainty in my workplace. As a leader, I have established a set-in-stone routine of what is expected at every hour of the day so that my team does not need to tiptoe into the office each morning wondering what to expect.

There are enough unpredictable obstacles that need to be over-come every day, so the importance of creating a healthy environment of consistency day in and day out removes unnecessary stress for my team, which means they can focus on what actually needs to get done. I don't want anyone worried about whether the boss is in a good mood that day. One great benefit of a consistent routine is that it creates a stable work environment, which increases productivity.

Another great benefit of consistency in both your personal life and work life is that it removes the possibility of inconsistent outcomes. All actions, choices, and behaviors lead to an outcome, and it is the outcome that ultimately makes the difference to the people around you.

For example, in my personal life, I have marked in my calendar two to three workout sessions a week that I commit to consistently. I have a healthy food shopping list that, no matter what, I buy weekly to ensure I have the proper ingredients or snacks for a consistently healthy lifestyle. I drink two glasses of water when I first wake up in the morning and then at least one glass with each meal, to ensure that without having to think about it, I have a consistent routine for the proper water intake.

Being consistent might seem like a small, trivial skill to work on and possess but I know I would not have achieved the same outcomes or reached the same level of success without it.

PUTTING IT INTO PRACTICE

KEY TAKEAWAYS:

- Consistency in your work performance builds trust and reliability in your team and lets your employers know what to expect from you.
- Making mistakes is human—be consistent in your resolution approach and take responsibility for your mistakes.
- Providing consistency in the workplace gives your team, employers, and stakeholders a sense of certainty, comfort, and security.
- Consistent habits eliminate inconsistent outcomes.

REFLECTION:

1. Think of what is serving you in your professional life. And with your team. How can you add consistency of communication in meetings: do you meet individually with each team member regularly, even for a few minutes and even when you do not have any urgent matter to discuss?
2. Do you have a daily meeting with your team to go over what each person is working on for the day or to identify roadblocks preventing anyone from moving forward?
3. What is working for you most in your professional life?
4. How consistent are you in your exercise regime? Is two to three times a week enough? Do you have an accountability calendar where you mark your sessions?
5. How consistent are your daily habits? Are you drinking eight glasses of water a day? How are your healthy eating habits? Are you stretching daily? Reading? Journaling?
6. What areas of your life would benefit from more consistency? Your workouts? Your relationships? Your health and wellness? Your professional settings? Your communication?
7. What would your new consistency strategy need to look like in both your personal and professional life to achieve your goals and dreams?

CHAPTER 10

Be Passionate

My friend and teammate for years, Benjamin, told me that when I give a presentation or participate in a meeting, there is such an undeniable magnetism and enthusiasm in the way I speak that sometimes the actual topic becomes irrelevant. The people watching my presentation get drawn in by my energy and excitement. This is because I am passionate about what I do, and I am proud of the work that I do.

> *"Every day, find something in your job, in your office, with your team, to get excited about and show that you care while you add value."*

We've all been in a job before that we don't completely love or that isn't our dream job. What I have done in that situation that others can't, won't, or don't do is find something about my job to be passionate about. That shift in mindset then completely changes the energy I bring to that role.

I take great pride in my work and my accomplishments, and that shows in how passionately I do my work. So, even if the job itself isn't what you love, make it something you can care about. Think of the big picture: If your goal is to become the best version of yourself in the workplace so that you can get that dream job, then, even if you are working in a job you don't like, strive to find passion in something that will increase how efficient you are as a worker, which will help you level up. It is that energy that will draw people to you and set you apart from your peers and may even help you develop the position you have into something else that is better, more appealing, or more fulfilling for you.

In terms of advancement, your superiors will be looking at candidates for promotion who not only work hard but who also have passion for the work they do. They don't want to fill higher positions with people who just get through the day-to-day, always caught up in thoughts about how they wish they had a better position. That kind of attitude really shows in your work ethic, quality of work, your energy levels, and your attitude.

Every day, find something in your job, in your office, with your team, to get excited about and show that you care while you add value to the organization. The passion I have had for my work over the years has given me a powerful edge over my peers as I've grown into leadership positions. It makes me more dedicated to my work, my success, and the success of my team. Ultimately, being passionate is a way to show that you care.

So, while others can't, won't, or don't get passionate about their work, empower yourself with an uplifting mindset of pride, care, and enthusiasm, and—most importantly—aim to help others in your team to succeed. You'll become a shining light to those around you, and it will garner attention from the right places while you work toward your goals.

Why Passion Is Important

Being in a leadership position means that your team is going to mirror your attitude and energy. If you are passionate about the work, your team will be too. Overall, this increases productivity and efficiency, but it also creates a more positive work environment. Imagine how different the office would feel if everyone on your team, including you, showed up each day with excitement to get started and enthusiasm to make progress. I intentionally try to show up as a caring, passionate person to my team, because I love what I do! The more I care, the more they will care—everybody wins!

I've found that when my team is passionate about their work, they will put more into it—not only will they be more focused throughout the day, but they will also look deeper for new and innovative solutions. They will participate more, and even go farther than expected, simply because they are enjoying themselves.

A great example is Peter, who used to work as a project manager in one of my teams. He was so passionate about his work and always went above and beyond. One day I saw him talking to and learning from his teammates. He ended up learning all the technical aspects of his teammate's job by being passionate about it, by offering help, and by being able to cover for his teammate during vacation.

It so happened that the teammate resigned and moved on. The technical position opened up and Peter got promoted. If he had never demonstrated this passion, he may never have learned from his friend, and the opportunity would have more likely gone to someone else. When you're a passionate leader, not only do you demonstrate that you care but you also pass that quality on to your team so that they too are passionate about their work. When you have a caring attitude, it encourages people to step outside their comfort zone and go to new levels with you as their support.

I have observed that when teams report to a manager or leader that is not engaged or passionate, they become disengaged. Why should a team care about a project if they feel their leader does not care? It is a well-known fact that when people feel they are nurtured and valued, they will do what they can to reinforce that value. In a work setting, that means they will work harder, be more dedicated, and continue to return excellent results. Your passion is a positive reinforcement to your team.

I saw this with an undergrad, Barbara, who started working as an assistant to the project managers in my team. She became passionate about the job and the potential growth it offered and always expressed how much she wanted to develop. She worked with consistency and discipline to showcase all her skills and before you knew it, she graduated from college. Today, she is an amazing and passionate project manager herself. And by the same token, she has taken others under her wing and trained them.

Passion might not seem as important as some of the topics in earlier chapters, but I can tell you, I would not have gotten to where I am today if I wasn't passionate about my work. It is that extra energy, touch of enthusiasm, and contagious magnetism that will set you, and your entire team, apart.

Outside of work, passion is just as important. Hopefully, in your personal life, it is easier for you to pick and choose activities or hobbies that you enjoy and get excited about. I encourage everyone to have at least one non-work-related hobby that they love to do and love to talk about that allows them to feel more energized and vibrant, be it art, dancing, music, cooking, gardening, hiking, camping, sewing, reading, fixer-upper projects...the list is endless!

As well as career success, it is also important to achieve personal success. Hobbies you are passionate about are a major part of personal success, because they increase your happiness, recharge or rejuvenate your emotional and mental energies, and are a huge part of self-care.

Get your team involved by asking them about hobbies they have outside of work. Encourage them to show off the fruits of their hobbies in the office—bringing in pictures to share, having a potted plant on their desk, hanging a painting they've done, etc. This kind of exchange is inspiring, helps you and your team connect, and promotes the pursuit of hobbies outside of work.

How to be Passionate About Anything and Everything

Let's be honest, there are times when you just might not feel like you can get passionate about something. But whether in your work or your personal life, a lack of passion and care will eventually have a negative impact on your happiness and your road to success.

What's to be done about it? This is how I look at it: If I'm not passionate about doing something, I try to see who this is benefiting and who I can provide value to through this task. In other words, this is my "Why." The feeling of giving has a positive effect on me, which makes me feel excited about what I do. My "Why" always involves helping others and adding value, which I can always be passionate about.

I remember when I had just accepted my expat assignment to China. Because of all the uncertainty—where I would live, what work would be like, what my day-to-day would look like—it was hard to get passionate about it. However, I found that focusing on how great this opportunity was and the reason why I had accepted it helped to ignite my passion and happiness about it. I decided to accept the post, not just because it was a savvy professional move and would give me great visibility in my organization but also because it would be an enriching experience for me learning a new area of the business as well as an opportunity for me and my daughter to immerse ourselves in a new language and culture. If you can't feel passionate about your current level of employment, find something in your day-to-day work that makes you happy and that you care about, and derive your passion from that. If you're like me and take pride in your accomplishments and focus on your small wins and on daily work-related accomplishments, they will give you the passionate drive to succeed overall.

PUTTING IT INTO PRACTICE

KEY TAKEAWAYS:

- Find something to be passionate about in everything you do.
- Passion overcomes uncertainty, fear, and negativity.
- When your team is passionate, they'll put their all into their work.

REFLECTION:

1. Find something in your work life to care about and be passionate about.
2. Think about what makes you happy and proud about your work or an outside-work activity and then transfer that over into areas of your life where you feel like you are lacking passion.
3. Break it down into smaller actions, and you'll find the balance you need to make yourself passionate about anything and everything.
4. What is your favorite hobby? What new hobby would you like to try?
5. Do you know your "Why?" Why do you like what you do for work? How can you help others to find their "Why?"

CHAPTER 11

Always Be Focused, Always Be Driven

Two great sayings I have learned and adopted for myself are: "Focus on what you can control," and "Be driven to be better today rather than tomorrow."

What a lot of people can't, won't, or don't do is remain focused and driven, whatever circumstances or negativity is thrown at them. It is easy to give up or get distracted, but you can achieve everything you want with the focus and drive to make it happen.

During the pandemic of 2020, one of the greatest barriers to success and productivity came in the form of idleness. As I mentioned in Chapter 5, I had former coworkers and acquaintances laid off due to the pandemic who then decided to remain unemployed even when new employment opportunities arose. Maybe they didn't want to start again, maybe they were making more money from the pandemic's unemployment benefits than what they'd make in a new job. Whatever the reason, they chose idleness, which is a really good way to get yourself stuck in one place and not move forward.

You can't achieve happiness and success through inaction. This is where being driven and having focus is going to be your asset, because developing these skills will ensure that you keep moving in the direction of what you want.

While I was fortunate enough to remain employed, I still faced significantly more down time than I had before the first few months of the pandemic. So, what did I do with my new free time? Well, I began coaching and mentoring others and started working on writing a book! It is my belief that, even when life slows down, I need to remain on point and focused on my goals. I looked for unusual opportunities that I hadn't had time for before but that I knew were things I wanted for my own happiness and my own success.

Even when it seemed like negative energy was closing in on me, I kept thinking, "What can I do to make myself better? What can I improve on for myself today?"

You might feel at times like you are being pulled in too many directions trying to balance work, home life, and your goals for success. If you ever feel that way, I recommend narrowing in on what helps you focus. What kind of incentives can you offer yourself to stick to your tasks, keep to your plans, and continue moving forward? In your home life it could be something like spending an hour with a good book, taking a bath, going for a walk with a friend, or a glass of wine at the end of the day. Think about what you are motivated to do the most—and the least. Then prioritize accordingly based on what you need to get done the most. Having a plan is a great tool to help you see what you want to achieve and how to get there, but you'll need to focus and have the drive to stick to it in order to accomplish what you want.

Incentives for focus and drive can be implemented with your team as well, helping them to keep their eyes on the prize at work. Not everyone responds to the same incentives, but in the workplace, I have found that most people appreciate praise for good work and positive reinforcement. I also tell my team to visualize what it will feel like when we achieve our goals.

Focus on What You Can Control

Focus goes beyond just remaining on task, especially in the work-place. Distractions can come from anywhere—kids, a spouse or romantic partner, thinking of where you want to eat out for dinner, etc. So, I look at it like this: When I go into work, I leave everything else at the door. When I come home from work, I leave everything else at the door. This mentality means that I will have the focus and energy to direct toward wherever I am and whatever I am doing. Even if working remotely, I make myself present in where I am and what my goals are at that time.

Most people, can't, won't, or don't create a clear division between these different aspects of their life. All it does is invite in distrac-tion, take away from productivity, create more stress and worry, and in the long run, hinder your chances of reaching your goals. I understand now, more than ever, it is harder to separate work life from home life when work *is* at home. However, to get around this, I separate areas of the house and set aside times in the day when I focus on one thing versus another to avoid distractions.

Adopting this viewpoint for yourself and encouraging your team to also keep that mindful focus will greatly eliminate outside distrac-tions and boost focus and productivity. With constant access to the internet, social media, cellphones, and everything else swirling around us daily, distractions are everywhere. So, start practicing leaving everything you don't need at the door if you work in an office, or in the other room, or at the desk.

Another important aspect of focus that too many people can't, won't, or don't do is focusing only on what they can control. Even as a team leader, you don't have control over the actions of your team members. Instead, focus on what motivation and encourage-ment you can offer to entice them to stay on track and do their best work.

In your home life, you don't have control over what people around you are doing, but you can take responsibility for yourself and your own actions, and even think about how what you do impacts others. You have control over your plan, your goals, and your actions. You have control over your own success and the results you get, whether that's work–life balance, health, or managing finances, so that is where your focus should be.

When it comes to your team, you might notice some members butting heads or always getting in each other's way. It is humbling, and a good reminder for your team, to go over what each person has control of. When you focus on what it is you can control, the things you can't control don't seem as worrisome anymore.

Be Driven to Be Better Today Rather than Tomorrow

I've been witness to a lot of people deciding that they will "be better tomorrow," or that they will "make the change tomorrow." What I do, that so many can't, won't, or don't do, is choose to be better *today.*

So, rather than putting things off for the next day, I choose to take action to be the best version of myself that I can be each and every day. I don't get stuck thinking, "Well if I can just get through this, I'll do better tomorrow." No, I learned at an early age from my mom that every single day counts. I tell myself, "I'm going to be the best today! And I will not leave for tomorrow what I can do today!"

When you think of putting something off to the next day, it becomes a habit to continuously put those things off. You need to adapt your thinking so that you want to be the best every day! This is a huge step toward accomplishing your goals, because being successful and being happy are in large part related to self-improvement and forward momentum. What better way to work toward self-improvement than work at being your best self, daily?

> *"You can't achieve happiness and success through inaction."*

Driving yourself to greatness will extend out into your work and personal life. It won't be enough for you just to feel great; you'll want to produce great work, be driven to reach your short- and long-term goals, and be driven to get those around you on the same path.

I've heard a lot of people talk about being driven in a negative way, as though it has to be exhausting and harsh. Leaders who appear driven can sometimes come off as pushy to their subordinates, as I know I did in the past. So be honest about why you're so driven and what it will lead you to achieve. I sometimes apologize to my team, as they know that I strive to be better every day and expect the same of them. However, you can be driven, and inspire that feeling in others, without pushing them or being too hard on them.

The best way to encourage others to follow is to really adopt the mantra: "Be better today rather than tomorrow." It is through those words that you can build productivity, eliminate procrastination, and foster a healthy mindset of not putting things off.

PUTTING IT INTO PRACTICE

KEY TAKEAWAYS:

- Focus on what you can control.
- Inaction leads to stagnation, which prevents opportunities and personal growth.
- Be driven to be better today rather than tomorrow.

REFLECTION:

1. Put a plan together to achieve your goals.
2. Set the daily tasks that you have to do in your calendar to avoid having to figure out what you need to accomplish each day.
3. As part of your morning routine, add a couple of questions: a) What can I do today to be better? b) What is something I need to accomplish today that I will not postpone to tomorrow?

CHAPTER 12

Be Direct! Boldness Is a Good Thing

Being direct has been a challenge for me as I have matured over the years. I like to tell my team that I am like wine, an acquired taste. I say this because I know I am direct. I am blunt and I am bold, but I balance it out with also being respectful. The way I see it is that, for me, being bold and direct is being authentic, but there is a way to do that while still respecting others or a person's rank, position, and how they might receive or react to what I say. Authenticity and transparency keep things focused and moving forward.

Honestly, what has ever been accomplished from beating around the bush? Other than stalling until you can gather the courage to be direct, it doesn't contribute to getting much done. When you practice being direct and bold, it becomes easier for you, and it also builds self-confidence and feelings of self-worth, which you are going to need for success!

What I do that a lot of people can't, don't, or won't do, is avoid the small talk, get to the point, and sometimes lead straight with the punchline. At times, I do get an awkward response from someone who isn't used to that kind of honesty, but I would argue that these reactions aren't bad or negative. The people I've worked with respond positively to honesty and transparency, because it leaves less room for error and tells them exactly where we stand with each other.

When I'm direct and honest, I get my point across in the most transparent way. My approach encourages immediate action, and I earn more active attention. When I say, "active attention," I mean I am noticed more, especially by my superiors. I set myself apart from my peers, and the higher-ups watch me to gauge what valuable skills I have. When I'm transparent, the people reporting to me have no room to misinterpret what I'm saying, what I'm asking of them, and what is required of them. When I'm transparent and direct with my superiors, they know exactly what I need or what I'm telling them—making their jobs easier in the long run.

I've gotten a lot of praise and respect from my superiors for being direct and bold. They know that I will be straight with them, that I will give them the facts, and that I won't try to sugar-coat anything that is a problem or not going the right way. However, this was an acquired technique that I learned with time.

Early in my career, I was too direct and had not yet honed the skill of being straightforward without stepping on anyone's toes. Not everyone could handle all business and no small talk at all. So, I learned to differentiate between team members' individual needs—I would continue to be direct, but I also understood that some people first needed a little bit of small talk and a personal connection. I'm not saying that I don't care about what is going on in everyone's personal lives when I am at work, but I believe that there is a time and place for everything and when it's grind time, you will find me getting down to business.

In the grand scheme of progress and success, by holding back, stalling, or trying to make things less serious, an entire project can be crippled if the reality of the situation is not fully expressed or embraced. I believe that there is an importance in bold directness for success, happiness, and progress. I also believe that when there are challenges, being direct about them helps improve not only the situation but also avoids the same challenges recurring.

Think of it this way: If you are not honest about what you want or are not direct with the people around you, you'll fall short of happiness every time. Directness and boldness come down to clear, transparent communication, and that is a necessary skill for getting what you want out of life. This is a technique that can be applied in both your professional and personal life.

Don't Be a Drill Sergeant

You can be direct without being mean. You can be bold without being harsh. It is all in the presentation. Honesty doesn't have to be brutal. At times, I struggled with being too harsh with my directness. As I became more experienced, I developed self-awareness in how I presented my honesty. Engaging in conversations completely listening to how people responded helped me overcome that harshness and default to respect instead. It is not always what we say, but how we say it.

When you're talking to other people, it is important to know your audience. In my experience, I've seen coworkers and friends be much more hesitant—beating around the bush—with their superiors, but then become much harsher with the people that answer to them—in other words, their team. You're a team leader, which means people look to you for direction, but that doesn't mean you have to bark orders at them all day long. This was one of the hardest skills for me to improve on as I am so direct that I always needed to remember to ensure I had empathy for others and was not hurting the other person's feelings.

There is a philosophy that a team's success is a direct reflection of their leader's ability to communicate and guide them. Take the military, for example. If the high-up generals aren't clear about their orders, the soldiers on the ground aren't going to complete their mission correctly. The military is also a good example of commanding officers yelling at their underlings for all kinds of things, even when the transgression is a direct result of poor leadership and a lack of direct communication.

Don't be a drill sergeant with your team! Say what you mean, mean what you say. Awareness of yourself and awareness of your audience are your greatest tools in being direct and bold without being mean and harsh.

Boldness in the workplace can manifest in many different ways. Being bold shows you are confident in yourself and in your work. When you believe in yourself and what you do, other people will notice and believe in you too. It is another way to prove your worth and potential to your leaders—bringing you that much closer to career success.

I've spoken with coworkers and people I've mentored that have told me they won't ask for things they want or need in the workplace. Either they don't want to inconvenience someone, or they think the answer will be "No," or they are simply insecure regarding how to go about having a direct conversation. For example, I once worked with a teammate who was new in a project team. She quickly became completely overwhelmed with all the tasks she had accepted, because she was insecure about saying "No" when asked if she could take something on.

Having worked in a project-oriented organization, I have seen teammates lacking the courage to be bold and tell their bosses which projects they want to work on. Equally, I have seen some ask and receive what they want. But being bold requires you to speak up and accept the value of failure, which many can't, won't, or don't do.

I always ask, "What's the worst that can happen if you speak up? They say 'No.'" Well, if you are already concerned about the answer being "No," then it won't be a disappointment. But, if the answer is something else, you can be proud that you've spoken up for yourself and gained something from it. Boldness, on an individual level, ties right back into taking a risk by daring to ask for something you worry will result in a negative answer. Greater rewards come from greater risks!

Directness and Boldness Move You Forward

Have you ever felt awkward when asking someone for a favor? It happens, and that awkwardness can lead to stalling and hesitation. If you stall and hesitate every time you need to express a want, need, or desire, you'll never achieve what you want the way you envisioned it, which will ultimately affect your personal happiness or success.

Here is an example: You live with your spouse or kids and want one of them to take out the trash every week. When you ask them, you aren't direct, and throw in tentative pleases, "If you wouldn't mind," and "If it's not an inconvenience." With that kind of indirectness, your request is easily interpreted as something that is optional for them to do.

On the flip side, if you were to say, "Can you please start taking the trash out to the curb every Wednesday night for a Thursday morning pickup?" the statement is direct, focused, and tells them exactly what you are asking for. You are not giving them a command or barking at them, and you are still cordial. Now, you've successfully freed up your Wednesday nights from chores!

Being bold yields results. Ask for what you want! Don't let fears or doubts prevent you from speaking up. You'll never know until you ask or speak out. I know, that's such a cliché, but it is a cliché because it is true!

Intention

I've learned to be intentional with my words and my conversations. This is slightly different from directness, but it is still a conscious form of communication and interaction that is an offset of directness. Before going into a meeting, I'll take a deep breath and think of the intention behind the meeting. I'll think of the intention of my pitch and why I chose to say what I have planned to say.

Prior to my team's weekly meetings, I think about the emotional goals I want to achieve. How do I want my team to feel at the end of the meeting? Especially during the pandemic when there is so much uncertainty, I wanted to make sure they felt it was a safe space to bring up any potential issues.

Being direct in my life comes with the purest of intentions. I want my team to know the reason I am not sugar-coating things is because when they do it right, they will learn, grow, and flourish. My goal is to always add value in the lives of those around me, and if I am always beating around the bush with my team or the people I work with, there may be room for misinterpretation and error. I want the best for my team and the most effective way I have been able to accomplish credibility, trust, respect, and success is by being direct.

When I focus on my intentions in a meeting, I can feel good about the experience the other participants are having. I won't get hung up on my emotions when I keep my intentions at the forefront of my focus. I can stick to what the meeting is about and how it is run without getting distracted.

Intentional conversation extends to daily interactions with my team, coworkers, and even my friends and family.

PUTTING IT INTO PRACTICE

KEY TAKEAWAYS:

- Being bold requires you to speak up and be prepared to accept failure.
- Be direct, but don't be mean or cruel.
- Practicing boldness builds self-confidence and increases your chances of coming into desired opportunities.
- You won't know until you ask. If you never boldly speak up for what you want, you won't know if you can get it, and no one will know what you want.
- Greater rewards come from greater risks.

REFLECTION:

1. Think of a conversation that you have been wanting to have but have hesitated about.
2. Imagine that you already have a bold mindset and that you are going to do what others do not expect from you.
3. Imagine that you are speaking to a close relative or friend, so you have no fear.
4. Address a difficult topic or tell someone "No" when they ask you for something.
5. If unsure, offer the other person two options (and both can be direct/bold options).
6. Take risks.
7. Own your results.

Only practice will allow you to feel confident and comfortable.

CHAPTER 13

Remember Your "Why"

You have probably been asked many times what you want to do in life or what your purpose in life is. If you have ever started a business or interviewed for a job you have probably heard this question: What is your "Why?" Why are you working toward a certain level of success? Why are you doing this one project? Why are you trying to get promoted? This basic "Why" question is paramount to setting achievable goals that add to your success and happiness.

In my life, understanding both my "Why" and my purpose has been a huge asset in achieving my own success and reaching my goals. If you find the process of trying to discover your "Why" overwhelming or frustrating, see if you can narrow it down to, "Why am I doing this?" or "Why am I trying to achieve X, Y, Z?"

Dean Graziosi is a real estate investor and author of the book *Millionaire Success Habits*. He is an innovator in the self-education industry and runs workshops on the subject. In one of these workshops, which I attended, he taught a method known as "peeling the onion," which he attributes to Dan Sullivan in his book (Graziosi, 2019). This is something that most people can't, don't, and won't do, but it helps you nail down your "Why." This is not about bringing tears to your eyes but simply about peeling back layers of a topic to know the reasoning behind our decisions to set up a specific goal.

Peeling the onion is a process of repetitively asking yourself questions and building up the answers until you get to the truth of the matter. To peel the onion, you ask yourself a "Why" question seven times about a specific idea, event, or ambition before setting a goal for it.

Here is an example:

What do you want to do in life? I want to make a lot of money.

Why do you want to have a lot of money? Because if I have a lot of money, I can take care of my family and travel the world.

Why do you want to take care of your family and travel the world? Because my family sacrificed a lot for me growing up and they always wanted to travel but couldn't afford it, so I want to be able to save up and explore the world with them.

Then, you do this four more times until your last reason is the deep epiphany of what you truly want out of life.

The biggest struggle people I've worked with have encountered is the frustration of setting a goal and not being able to meet it. This frustration can lead to you putting off making goals in the future. I no longer encounter this scenario, because now I always know my "Why," and I can share my reasoning clearly with those around me about my goals for success. However, it took me years to figure this out. I used to set up goals to meet others' expectations regarding my professional goals, my body weight goals, and even my relationship goals. And then what happened? I'd fail at achieving my goals!

Nowadays, I set my goals according to the highest priorities in my life. This focus fuels my commitment to achieving my goals, but I would not be able to set such focused goals without knowing my purpose, my true "Why." To maximize my likelihood of success, I have a sense of urgency, an "I must do this" attitude, because I know my purpose and have created specific goals that are important to my career, my wellbeing, and my relationships.

"In my life, understanding my 'Why' and my purpose has been a huge asset in finding my own success and reaching my goals."

Without unlocking this mindset, you are more likely to put off what you need to both set and reach a goal, which leads to frustration and demotivation. You can end up in an "I can't do anything or be successful at anything" mindset, which will only damage your chances at reaching success and happiness.

By utilizing the peeling the onion method, I built up my "I must do this" attitude, giving me the energy and drive to succeed where other people in that situation would fall flat or burn out. It was through doing this exercise that I discovered why I wanted to write this book, share my experiences, and allow myself to be vulnerable so others can learn from my experiences and stories.

Why Did I Set This Goal?

The peeling the onion method can also be used to analyze whether or not a goal is still serving your overall desires. As I said in Chapter 2, you're going to want to revise and revisit your goals and plans often so that they continually align with where you see yourself going. So, when you are setting up goals, leverage the exercise, and ask the question "Why?" seven times to uncover the truest answer to why you want to achieve them.

If you ever feel like a goal isn't leading you to success, or that you aren't able to follow through on a plan, or like a skillset is no longer needed or valuable, ask yourself, "Why?" Use the peeling the onion exercise to get a deeper understanding of why it is no longer serving you. If you can't remember why you set a specific goal in the first place, then it is probably no longer aligned with your desires or ambitions for success.

Knowing your "Why" in relation to your career and work setting helps give you clearer direction. When you have clear direction, you can point your team in that same, clear direction. You'll then be able to find opportunities for advancement and have open discussions about what else you can contribute to.

I revisit my goals weekly, and if I don't have a clear "Why," I utilize the peeling the onion method to reorganize them and redirect my focus. I'd recommend bringing this same approach to your team and making it standard practice. Teach it to them as a goal-building and goal-revising tool, for teamwide goals and individuals' career and personal life goals.

Am I Off Course?

I've seen a lot of people set intermediate goals for themselves that are off course from their long-term plans or desires. This is the result of not having clarity in what they want or where they want to go.

Being off course can become incredibly frustrating because you can see what you desire but can't reach it. You're still setting and reaching lots of small goals, but it feels like nothing will get you want you want, because you don't realize the small goals you've set are off course and therefore cannot get you to where you need to be: a vicious cycle that can only be broken with more clarity into your Why.

I've also seen people set goals for themselves, and then take steps that actively lead them off course from their goal. If you set actionable steps that don't align with your goal, you'll never get there. It can become a constant uphill battle of trying and trying without ever feeling like you've accomplished anything.

The peeling the onion method can be used in both these situations to get to the meat of the issue, so to speak. As a team leader, make goal revision and peeling the onion regular parts of your routine. The more you do it, the easier it becomes, and the less time it takes.

Being off course might feel natural at times, or sometimes we do not realize we are off course until a situation makes us question our "Why." I know this from the time when I got a new job as a consultant at a small, fast-growing firm. The work seemed right up my alley, but there were a few red flags: I had not heard great stories about the culture of the company, and I had my doubts about the work environment. I had a funny feeling about it, but I still decided to take the job, even though I was not convinced I had made the right decision.

A few months after working there, Bianca, my daughter, got hurt playing flag football in school when a kid hit her in the nose. The school called me to go get her immediately as she would not stop bleeding.

Obviously in a hurry and about to leave, I told the CEO the situation—that my daughter needed me to take her to the ER. His response: Couldn't you get someone else to go pick her up? In that moment, not only I was flabbergasted but I realized the leader of this company did not care about me as his employees. I felt completely off course. I questioned myself, "Is this really where I want to grow? Do I feel fulfilled in this company?" Within days I had quit because after I identified my "Why," I realized that working there was not serving me. I also learned from my actions: I wanted to make sure as a leader I would always be careful and, more importantly, caring about how I react to an employee having a family emergency.

It is important to check in with your team from time to time to see if they are comfortable with their goals and the progress they are making toward them. This is true of their career goals and any personal goals they are comfortable discussing in a work setting, or even if they want an accountability partner or a mentor. Encourage them to come to you with questions or concerns about meeting or revising their goals and help them set up a plan for revision, going through the steps of peeling the onion for more clarity.

PUTTING IT INTO PRACTICE

KEY TAKEAWAYS:

- Ask yourself "Why" regularly.
- Re-evaluate your "Why" regularly.
- Make sure your goals and actions are serving your greater purpose.

REFLECTION:

You will need sticky notes, a pen, and a few large sheets of paper.

Exercise One: Figure out which goals to work on.

1. Decide if you want to do this exercise for your professional or personal goals, or both at the same time.
2. Think of all the goals you have. On each sticky note, write ONE goal only—yes, just one. An urge to write more than one would clearly show that you are trying to achieve too many goals at once—and why you are not achieving them.
3. Take the sheet of paper and draw three concentric circles like this:

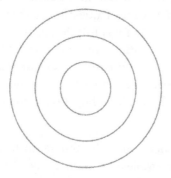

4. In the inner circle, place the goals that are closest to your heart: that you love, that bring you joy, that are must do's because they utilize your talents. The ones that align with your vision, desires, and passion.
5. In the middle circle, place the ones that you would be very happy to achieve but wouldn't be crushed not to.

6. In the outer ring, place those that you dread, the ones that drain your energy, the ones that have been imposed on you by others, by peer pressure.
7. When all your sticky notes are arranged in the circles, you need to think hard about your "Why" for choosing each goal and decide to eliminate the activities or goals that are in your outer circle so you can focus on the inner circle and focus your energy on achieving those goals.

Exercise Two: Peeling the onion to know your "Why."

Asking deeper questions is the key to finding out the true answers that really matter.

1. Get another sheet of paper and pick one of the goals you put in the inner circle from the above exercise. Write this goal at the top of the paper.
2. Then, put a #1 and underneath your goal, write the first question: "**Why** do I want to make this a goal?" Draw a line from it and write down the answer.
3. Ask question #2: "**Why**?" Draw another line from this one and write the answer.
4. Ask question #3: "**Why?**" and continue to add the lines, and your answers, until you get to seven **Why's** from your original question.

This exercise goes several layers deep, enabling you to get to the real answer to your question: "Why," and the purpose or reasoning behind your goals.

*Make yourself persistently ask yourself "**But why**..." You may be amazed with your discoveries.*

CHAPTER 14

Have Upward Conversations

W hat I do that most people can't, don't, or won't do is manage my boss's expectations through what I call "upward conversations," so that there are no surprises and meeting expectations leads to success. In addition, during these conversations we create opportunities to provide feedback, can discuss any suggestions to improve, or even any potential dissatisfaction with areas of the job that may not be working. These conversations are ways to get to know each other and help you to anticipate your boss's needs, offer solutions, and be the most effective employee that you can be.

> *"Having upward conversations isn't sucking up. It is about being real with your boss."*

I've worked with and mentored a lot of people that are stuck with this idea that their boss is someone to fear, or that they should just stay out of their boss's way. Respecting someone does not mean staying away or avoiding having healthy, challenging conversations. I've taught them that to really stand out, you want to be in your boss's way, but positively and respectfully.

You want to talk to your boss about their expectations and be transparent with them about how you and your team will manage those expectations. This includes letting them know what will work, what won't, what will get done, and what areas need more support or more time, and so on.

Not only does this directness give you more face-to-face time with your boss, but it also shows that you are well versed in managing your own team or leading others and that you understand their work capabilities. You also demonstrate that you are honest. You will establish credibility with your boss when you don't just say, "Yes, of course I can do that," even while you have doubts in the back of your mind.

Committing to a goal, project, or deadline just because your boss asked you to and you're too worried to say "No" leads to a stressful situation for you and your team and could even backfire if the goal or project isn't completed in time or as expected; Neither of which are aligned with happiness or success.

As a team leader, you are probably already in a management position, so using skills we've discussed in previous chapters, like directness and risk management, will help you to better manage your boss's expectations and communicate with them clearly.

This is a "take charge" attitude that I've always practiced in the workplace, and you could try it too. Any leader likes their team members to have a "can do" attitude that helps them get ahead of their workload and which makes their own role a little easier.

Going one step further, anticipating the needs of your boss will make you stand out even more as a manager or leader that is already ahead of the game. It is a great quality to understand the inner workings and needs of the company you work for—it shows that you are a "go-getter," and that you know and respect your boss and superiors.

Having a Positive Relationship with Your Boss

You should build a positive relationship with your boss. That's kind of obvious, isn't it? Well, when I say a positive relationship, I don't just mean be on friendly terms, I mean embracing positive communication, openness, and a peer-to-peer working relationship.

Just like you, your boss is a manager, an employee, a family member, and a part of the company you both work for and is trying to balance it all just like we all do.

Your boss is responsible for your raises, promotions, recommendations, approving additional responsibility, etc. When you build a personal relationship—and a positive one—with them, you stand out as an effective and high-profile employee. Your boss will think of you when new opportunities arise and will already be comfortable with your work potential.

I learned this after many bosses and many years. If I had focused on building this relationship earlier, I would have probably grown at a faster rate in my career with my bosses supporting my career path. I say this because I learned the hard way that in many companies in corporate America, when you want another position, even one in a different department, often your boss will be consulted and will give the recommendation or approval for you just to be considered for that position. So, having a great relationship with your boss is key to you climbing the ladder.

Having upward conversations isn't sucking up. It's about being real with your boss. It's about giving them what they need while at the same time expressing what you need, or in other words, looking out for your boss's needs while also managing your and your team's needs. When you manage expectations, you usually meet them!

Let me give you an example. I once took over a multimillion-dollar data center renovation when another project manager had failed at delivering it. I was under a lot of pressure, and everyone was unhappy. After doing an assessment, I had a bold and clear conversation with my leaders. I explained that I could deliver the project, but it would be delivered three days after their expected deadline, and instead of all ten areas working, only nine would work on that day, with the remaining one following a day later. Even though it took a lot of courage to announce this plan and garnered dissatisfaction at the time, ultimately, when the whole project was delivered—even with the delay—it was all perceived as a success on my part. Why? Because I managed expectations in the beginning.

As a team leader, you are in a very powerful position, situated between a team of hard workers who may be very close to the products or services provided, and the higher-ups. You have the ear and the attention of both sides of the workforce—you need to know how to capture it and keep it.

Having upward conversations is more than just building a good relationship with your boss. It is also about strengthening existing relationships and about becoming more comfortable with expressing yourself and your needs while also acknowledging someone else's. It means looking out for the wellbeing of someone else while also looking out for your own needs. Share your own stories and let others know you understand their experiences. It is okay to be human and make the relationship personal. You do not need to be an ironman or woman of steel.

Upward conversations build your confidence, show your greater potential, and make you stand out to others while consolidating a positive relationship with your boss.

Being confident carries over into all areas of your life, leading to a clearer picture of what you want and what will make you happy, with the additional certainty of being able to achieve it.

There are many benefits of having upward conversations: they keep you in your boss's line of sight at all times and make you a more effective team leader; they open up opportunities; and they build healthier, happier relationships that can save you time and lead you to success in your career.

Have a Voice at the Table—How I Did It

One time, new in a position I had just started, I was called into a meeting about a new project plan with the company VP and many other executives and peers. I'd done my homework on the meeting topic and had all the information laid out. During the meeting, as everyone discussed the project, they all seemed to be in agreement.

I was the only one that spoke out and said I thought their approach would fail. Everyone looked at me like I was speaking out of place and was clearly wrong. After all, I was the newest member of the team, what could I possibly know? They went ahead with their execution of the plan. Perhaps it wasn't my best first impression...

However, a week later when things didn't work out, the VP called another meeting and asked me, in front of everyone, how I could have known the project would fail. I replied that prior to the previous meeting I had spoken to key engineers and architects and realized that the product's integration with other systems had not been fully figured out and resolved. Essentially, by speaking up, I gained the respect and trust of my boss and my colleagues. If you know you've done the work and are confident in your assessments, don't be afraid to share them.

This one instance opened a lot of doors for me. I had proven that I did all the background research I needed, and even though I was new, I'd showcased my abilities as a competent team member early on, gaining trust and respect much faster. I encourage everyone who puts in the work and feels confident about it not to be afraid and to bring their voice to the table!

PUTTING IT INTO PRACTICE

KEY TAKEAWAYS:

- Be real with your boss.
- Understand and anticipate your boss's needs for a more fluid, efficient relationship.
- Have your own voice at the table.
- Don't be afraid to speak up.
- Ask for what you want.

REFLECTION:

1. Set up a time to talk to your boss.
2. Suggest you schedule regular meetings.
3. In your next discussion, take a moment to connect personally. Do not assume your boss knows everything you are working on, so bring notes that cover:
   - What was accomplished in the last week/month
   - What challenges you and team encountered and overcame
   - What you and your team are working on next
   - What could go wrong and your plan to overcome those challenges

CHAPTER 15

Think Outside the Box

I know, I know, thinking outside the box sounds like a business cliché, but I promise you that it isn't! The point of clichés is that they have a good basis of truth in them. I always try to think outside the box or, honestly, I ignore the box, because it lets me approach problems from different angles, without boundaries, without limits, and with new perspectives.

Being a common cliché has, perversely, made it something that a lot of people can't do, won't do, or don't do anymore. If you want to get ahead and show that you are a valuable employee and leader, start thinking outside the box. Especially when you or your team are implementing something new and things get tough or when someone tells you something cannot get done. It is those innovative ideas that really set you apart. I believe that nothing is impossible and so should you!

The proverbial box is a very narrow, closed space. Once you look outside of it, you can find innovative solutions. That's why I will take the broadest perspective possible so I can find solutions hidden behind the rocks.

But it is not just about coming up with amazing, creative, and unique ideas. You also want to build on and encourage the ideas that your team comes up with when they are merely feasible. Sometimes the best solutions are the simplest and thinking outside the box or without limits can help you realize that you don't always need bells and whistles. Transforming a good idea into a great solution is a powerful way to set yourself apart.

I still encourage my team to think outside the box every day. Not only does it promote new ideas and perspectives, but it keeps your team involved and engaged, gives them freedom to tackle problems, and encourages them to speak up and present their ideas.

Thinking outside the box is about conceptualizing ideas differently. This works best when you have the whole team involved and everyone contributing. So, even though we do not implement every idea that is brought up, no idea is criticized, as I do not want to stop the team from bringing new ideas to the table.

Remember, not everything has to be done the same way over and over again. When you do this, you get yourself, and your team, stuck in a rut. It is why I'm always asking my team to voice their suggestions on how to improve what we do, automate any processes, and think of new methods of doing things.

Another benefit of having your whole team think outside the box is that they can bring in suggestions and ideas that you might not have previously considered. Remind your team often that if they have an idea, you want to hear it. What is the worst thing that could happen when they speak up? The idea isn't selected or used. That doesn't mean it isn't valid or shouldn't be presented.

By thinking outside the box, my bosses have trusted me to come up with good, unique solutions from a perspective outside their own. They know my abilities, and they know that I am willing to try new things in order to get the best results.

Be an Innovator

Even though it is an overused phrase, when you think outside the box to solve challenges —or think there is no box—you'll be considered an innovator. A lot of the greatest advancements in technology and business have been accomplished through innovative ideas.

Be an innovator! You want to build the reputation for yourself as a creative thinker. This does not mean you need to create new and innovative products—it could be you learn how to implement something in an innovative way. My team knows me as someone who thinks laterally and wants to hear and implement different and unique suggestions from them.

> *"Remember, not everything has to be done the same way over and over again."*

Thinking outside the box not only bolsters confidence and develops problem-solving skills, but it has given me an edge as I'm known as someone who can get things done! This comes from figuring out how to get things done and finding creative solutions when others may think it is impossible and just give up.

Be a creator! When you're innovative and think outside the box, you don't just go with the flow. Going with the flow is easy and safe. When you challenge the status quo, you create the outcome and solutions rather than ride along the easy path.

Thinking outside the box is a "must have" when you are striving for success in your career. It is equally as important a skill to have if you want success and happiness in your personal life too.

Any time an innovative, out-of-the-box solution makes sense, I'd recommend using it even if other people might second guess your proposal. Get comfortable with trying new things by falling back on your risk-analysis skills from Chapter 3 to weigh the options and mitigate the risks. When you trust yourself and your decision-making abilities, you'll trust yourself to choose the right, innovative options.

If I had all the Money and Time in the World...

Sometimes I think to myself, "If I had all the money and time in the world, how would I accomplish this goal differently?" It is a pretty big extreme, but removing time and money constraints allows me to jump into a perspective outside my current situation. The "box" that we are all expected to fit into limits creativity and individuality. Sometimes that works, but to find the success and happiness that you want, you'll have to move beyond it. For example, when planning a vacation, it's easier to buy "off-the-peg" and end up seeing only the parts of a new city or country that everyone else will see on their tried and tested tourist trail. Instead, I like to buy some literature and go online to research a new place and find hidden gems for me and my family to discover that others would miss entirely because they couldn't, wouldn't, or didn't think creatively about their trip.

In a professional context I try to free up my mind to go beyond what I think I can do, and this opens the lid to the proverbial box. This question removes limits and takes me to a place outside my current thought patterns.

Use this same thought pattern for yourself and ask your team this question too. You'll discover that without the limitations, everyone will come up with unique ideas that are different from yours and different from each other's. Suddenly, you'll have a lot to choose from, which ensures that you and your team can come up with the best ideas and solutions.

Any problem, project, or challenge can be resolved with a little out-of-the-box thinking. Encourage your team to bring this limit-removing question into their personal lives too, because it will greatly increase their personal productivity, problem-solving skills, and overall happiness.

PUTTING IT INTO PRACTICE

KEY TAKEAWAYS:

- Think outside the box—think, "How would I do this?" and "If I had all the time and money in the world, what would I do?"
- Free your thoughts to come up with innovative solutions and ideas.
- Remember that not everything has to be done the same way over and over again.
- Be an innovator!

REFLECTION:

1. Think of a problem you are trying to solve.
2. Imagine you have all the money and time in the world to solve it.
3. If you were to challenge something about the status quo, what would that be?
4. What comes to mind as different and potential solutions?
5. Narrow these down to three solutions.
6. Revisit the risk-analysis exercise from Chapter 3—do a risk analysis of your options.
7. Make a plan and set out actions to reach your goal and solve the problem.

CHAPTER 16

If You Don't Know Something, Learn It

We live in a world where we are so dependent on others. How do you do this? What does that mean? Can I make this? I say, if you don't know, FIGURE IT OUT! With the technology we have at our fingertips, everything can be learned with relatively little effort. We just have to unlock our mindsets and understand that if you don't know something, just learn it.

It might be easier said than done, but there have been times throughout my career where a certain skillset or knowledge is required for a job or project, and no one has been available with that knowledge. When this happens, I take it upon myself to learn what needs to be learned. Of course, this does not mean that if an engineer is not available you just start to code, or if the surgeon is on vacation you start operating. I just try to be resourceful.

Sometimes I can find an expert in my field who has the sought-after skill, as discussed in Chapter 6, but every now and then the person I need just isn't there. So, when this happens, what is to be done about it? What I do that a lot of people can't, won't, or don't do is learn the skill or knowledge for myself using whatever resource I have.

> *"There is an endless wealth of knowledge out there, and when you research new things, you develop skills that you didn't even know were related to the topic."*

I dive into research mode, pick up a book, go online, or take a crash course and I take up the responsibility of equipping myself with the information I need. This sets me apart from my peers as someone who gets stuff done, but also someone who is willing to expand my knowledge base and skillset to always accomplish my projects.

It also gives me the chance to become a subject matter expert on a topic that few other people at my job, if any, are knowledgeable about. This increases my value as an employee and makes me approachable to those seeking advice and information about that topic.

I believe that it is important for you to always look to expand your skillset and raise your own bar because you never know when these new skills will become essential to your success.

Just after I moved to California in the year 2000, during the dotcom era, I applied for a job at a telecommunications company that was looking for a project management team to work on planning R&D projects. The need for someone with Excel skills was essential, however I was far from being proficient in Excel. I didn't want to miss out on the opportunity of getting this job, so in the interview, I clearly emphasized how quick a learner I was and stressed that I was more than capable of using Excel even though I knew I was going to have to brush up on learning...well, almost everything about Excel. In the end I got that job and took all kinds of courses and became an Excel formula guru before my first day.

This is about taking initiative and becoming resourceful. You never want to tell your boss, "I didn't get that done because I didn't know how," or "No one on the team had the right skillset to accomplish that." Instead, be the "go-getter" and take on a little extra responsibility to see it through. Of course, unless you can hire for the skillset.

I've seen employees choose to take the stance of: "Well, someone else will figure it out." Don't be that person! Don't be the one that consciously turns down the chance for personal growth. Be the one who says: "If no one else knows what is needed, I'll figure it out." Whenever you are faced with this situation, see it as an opportunity for self-improvement, growth, and expansion—which all lead to greater things for yourself and your goals.

This mentality of being prepared to learn something new is not just specific to becoming more efficient and productive in your career—it gives you the skills to succeed where others can't, won't, or don't in your personal life too. Ever wanted to learn how to make bread? Well, read about it. Want to know how to build yourself a bookcase? Research it, get the materials, and get it done! There is an endless wealth of knowledge out there, and when you research new things, you develop skills that you didn't even know were related to the topic.

Going back to the bookcase, if you were to learn how to build a bookcase, you'd also be learning how to follow a construction plan, measure, cut, and use a multitude of tools to create something. Those skills aren't exclusive to building a bookcase, so now you've expanded your skillset far beyond your initial goal and into general carpentry!

The same is true when you bring new knowledge to your career. Accumulating skills adds to your proficiency, productivity, efficiency, and value as an employee and as a team leader. In the age of technology, there are no excuses for not learning new things because so much information is available right at your fingertips. Literally—on your computer, on your tablet, and on your smartphone.

All skills that relate to your work projects and tasks will add value to you as an employee. Even if the job you have now isn't the career you want long term, growing your skills at this level will only help you as you move up the ranks or change industries.

I don't believe there are any useless skills or knowledge. Everything has a purpose and a reason, so when you find yourself faced with a talent, skill, or knowledge gap at work, fill it in yourself! You never know how new skills will benefit you later on, so there is no point in turning away from the opportunity—instead, lean into it to learn and grow.

The Value of Teaching Others

Part of bringing new knowledge into your workplace is teaching others and adding value to the lives of the individuals you are surrounded with each day. When you learn a new skillset to improve your own work, pass it along to your team. As a manager or executive, you should always be looking for ways to improve your team's productivity and efficiency. Passing along new knowledge and skills is a great way to do that!

You'll be seen as the source of the knowledge—the subject matter expert and the "go-to" person if anyone has any questions—and your team will benefit from having new skills to use and their own expert right nearby! You will be surprised how the process of sharing skills will translate into more knowledge for you, because as your team members learn from you and expand their knowledge themselves, they will in turn share it with you and the team.

The game-changer tip that I teach my teams is to adopt this same mindset of figuring out solutions for yourself. If you don't know something, learn it. When you do, don't be greedy—share it with your teammates. Imagine how successful your team will become when applying these two golden gems:

1: Be proactive and research the things you don't know.

2: Share what you learned with your team.

When I worked as a consultant years ago, I used to think that if I kept my knowledge to myself, it would translate into job security. However, as time passed and I matured, I learned that the more knowledge I shared, the more respected and in-demand as a consultant and as an employee I became.

Bringing new information to your team will set you apart from other managers and executives that can't, won't, or don't teach their team new things. I've said it before, and I'll say it again: When working toward your own success, your team's abilities are going to reflect greatly on that. You are in the best position to grow their skills, which brings the team together and gets everyone involved.

Additionally, by taking on the role of mentor with your team and by taking the initiative to learn new things for the benefit of your team and the company as a whole, you will get noticed in different ways. This opens up two different avenues of opportunity.

First, as a mentor. I've always liked to share my knowledge and coach others, and I'm proud to say I have been able to improve people's careers and guide them to the next level. I've mentored several recent college grads, entrepreneurs, and high performers in corporations by using the skillset that I have shared in this book, for example, by helping them increase or hit a six-figure salary in a short time frame. Those successes led me to write this book and continue to spread my knowledge and skills.

> *"Bringing new information to your team will set you apart from other managers and executives that can't, won't, or don't teach their team new things."*

Second, in my personal life. Teaching others isn't limited to your career. In your day-to-day activities with friends, family, and other interpersonal relationships, if you have knowledge, don't be afraid to share it at the appropriate times. This can lead to satisfying bonding experiences, creating stronger relationships and some very enjoyable, if not humorous, memories.

Your own success and happiness might not be rooted in teaching others, but it is a good way to improve relationships, add value to other people's lives, and overall have some fun, which will, in the long run, help you reach your goals of success and happiness.

PUTTING IT INTO PRACTICE

KEY TAKEAWAYS:

- There is an endless wealth of information out there. Be proactive and research the things you don't know.
- Bringing new information and sharing it with your team will set you apart from other managers and leaders.
- When you research new things, you develop new skills that you didn't even know were related to the topic.
- Teach and encourage others to broaden their skillsets.

REFLECTION:

Learning new skills:
1. What skills would help you do your job better and more easily?
2. How can you acquire those skills?
3. Go for it!

Sharing knowledge:
1. What areas of expertise are you sought after for?
2. What skills do you have that your team can benefit from learning from you?
3. What would it take to share or teach anyone in your organization your skills?
4. Think of the benefits that will bring to you and them.
5. Be open to sharing your knowledge and let others learn from you!

CHAPTER 17

Step Outside Your Comfort Zone

J ob descriptions are overrated. There, I said it! When you come across a job description that you don't feel qualified for, I recommend that you apply anyway. (I'm obviously referring to jobs that are in the realm of your skillset.) Job descriptions are not always the true reflection of what the hiring manager is looking for, so apply and see if you get an interview! What's the worst that could happen? You don't get the job. You have nothing to lose and everything to gain because if you do get the job, you could completely transform your career!

What so many people can't, won't, or don't do is step outside their comfort zone. They limit themselves with their own doubts and fears instead of pushing beyond the boundaries they've put in place. Yes, I know, this might be another thing to add to the list of clichéd tips, but I'm here to ask those who have heard this a million times before, have you truly put this into practice? How far out of your comfort zone have you really pushed yourself?

Don't hold yourself back with doubts like, "I'm not qualified," or "There are better suited applicants applying." These limiting thoughts can cause you to miss some great opportunities.

Instead, think positively. Think, "I won't know unless I apply," or "This is a good chance for me to take," or even, "It is low risk, but high reward, so I'm going to do my best."

When I made the decision to leave the medical field and enter the technology field, I knew I wanted to move to Silicon Valley even though I had no experience in technology. I still did it! Back then, companies used to have open houses, so I showed up and waited at the lobby of a tech firm for an interview, and I waited for several hours before anyone gave me the time of day to see what skillset I had to offer and what asset I could be to them.

I had given them my résumé upfront and I knew a couple of people at the company that tried to put a word in. They were aware of my background and, of course, as my résumé did not have any technology experience, I knew nobody would want to give me an interview. Plus, at the time, telecommunications was a male-dominated industry. But if you have learned anything about me in this book by now, you can best believe that I stayed all day waiting for an opportunity to speak to someone—anyone.

My perseverance paid off—and I most definitely felt out of my comfort zone—when someone saw that I had been waiting in the lobby all day and asked, "What are you still doing here?" I told him I was waiting for someone to give me the chance of interviewing and that I was not going to leave without at least discussing the opportunities of a job.

The man saw the ambition in my eyes, my perseverance, and the determination I held in my shoulders, which must have counted for something because after eight hours, six restroom breaks, and four cups of coffee, I was finally granted an interview! Let's just say that after that one interview, I was hired. I had no previous experience in technology, and I didn't have a lot of what the job description had outlined, but I still went for it, and it totally paid off! It was the breakthrough point in my career change that pulled me out of the medical industry and gave me a foothold in the technology field.

> *"When you get too comfortable, you stop looking for new opportunities, risks become 'too risky' no matter what they are, and everything becomes about maintaining that sense of comfort. Do you see how this is counterproductive toward success?"*

Making a good first impression can open the door to opportunities that you believe you qualify for. That was what I faced. Even before that tech company interviewed me, they noticed my perseverance, my determination, my ability to take risks and try something new, and my willingness to start over in a whole new industry and put the hard work in.

This is why I say job descriptions are overrated, because you never know what qualities and skills of yours are going to win the hearts and minds of the people you interview with. After all, we still interview with human beings. If the reward outweighs the risk, there is no reason not to take the chance.

Sometimes, it isn't just about your qualifications, it's about your williness in taking a risk, trying something new, and yes, stepping outside your comfort zone. So many people get comfortable in a safe space that they can't, won't, or don't ever leave that space. Don't let yourself get stuck in a certain job or position just because it is comfortable.

Success and happiness come from advancement and personal growth. You can't grow if you stay in the shade, too afraid to step into the sun because it is new and unfamiliar.

Have You Heard of Impostor Syndrome?

Impostor syndrome is defined as the feeling someone gets when they "doubt their abilities and feel like a fraud" in their position (Burey and Tulshyan, 2021). It disproportionately impacts high-achievers and their ability to accept what they've accomplished, questioning whether or not they deserve what they've achieved.

I've worked with and coached several people that have confessed to having impostor syndrome, or who feel underqualified for the work they do. Essentially, they are unable to accept their accomplishments.

What I always tell them is this: "Don't let impostor syndrome hold you back. Just like other people can do the job, you are also capable of doing the job! Believe in yourself!"

You are fully equipped to perform any job or task at the same level as anyone else. What sets the successful people apart from the mediocre or mid-level is that they put the work in. They step out of their comfort zone, take risks, challenge themselves, and educate themselves to always get the job done. Anyone and everyone is capable of doing this.

Becoming confident within yourself and acknowledging your value, your skills, and your ability to grow is paramount to your ability to achieve the success that you want. It is in being self-confident that you are also able to accept compliments and feel like you are qualified for the position you are in.

This is true in your personal life as well. When you become confident with who you are—your skills, your appearance, your goals, and aspirations—you feel worthy of achieving them and garnering praise for what you accomplish.

To me, impostor syndrome is just another term for low confidence and not realizing your value or your worth. Be confident in who you are, what you want, and in knowing that you are capable of doing what needs to be done for any career path or goal you've set for yourself.

Sometimes, it takes a little extra work, but what will set you apart from so many others is actually doing the things that scare you, challenge you, and are outside of your comfort zone.

In your position as manager or executive, you should do your utmost to encourage your team to overcome impostor syndrome if you notice they are experiencing it. You can do this by regularly offering praise and positive reinforcement where it is due and by ensuring that the person understands they are deserving of it.

If anyone on your team has low confidence or seems to think they are underqualified, try some team activities that help boost confidence overall. You could even ask them directly why they don't feel qualified to accomplish certain tasks. If it is a matter of skillset and knowledge, provide additional material for them to research or go over so they feel like they have a better grasp of what is needed to perform in their position.

When you build your team's confidence, their work quality, efficiency, and attitude improve. Not only does this reflect positively on you, but it also creates a more invigorating, uplifting, and productive work environment.

Why Safety and Security Aren't Always Beneficial to Success

It is human nature to want to feel a sense of safety and security, especially when it comes to a solid career. Financial security is a major benefit for a lot of people and informs their decisions regarding their personal lives, where they want to live, career-based choices, etc.

When it comes to advancement, success, and personal growth, the need for safety and security can turn into pitfalls and roadblocks. Certainly, feeling safe and secure is comfortable. But comfort can so easily become stagnation.

That is why I say stepping out of your comfort zone is so important! When you get too comfortable, you stop looking for new opportunities, risks become "too risky" no matter what they are, and everything becomes about maintaining that sense of comfort. Do you see how this is counterproductive toward success?

Any time you come up against something that feels too risky or too uncomfortable, complete a full risk analysis and management plan for it. Don't just give up on it before it is even fully thought out. For example, try taking small steps out of your own comfort zone by trying something new at work. It doesn't have to be extreme, but it will always be impactful. Whether you succeed and learn a new skill or method to work with, or it doesn't go so well, at least you will be left with a learning experience. You gain something either way, most importantly that you can step outside your comfort zone without that safety and security disappearing.

Most of the time, if someone is too comfortable to take a perceived risk, they just need a little push to show them that it isn't the end of the world. If you have anyone on your team that has a specific comfort zone, try assigning them tasks that will coax them out of it, one step at a time.

You don't want to push too much, too fast, but with a nudge you can completely change their mentality. This brings more innovative "go-getters" to your team that are confident and who become valuable assets.

I do a rotation of roles in my team. I have implemented this in several teams and mostly, at the beginning, some folks who are too comfy in their roles hate the idea of stepping out of their comfort zones. The most important thing is to coach, encourage, and support them throughout.

A rotation allows you to have a team where it does not matter who goes on vacation or wins the lottery and leaves, because anyone can pick up the workload. In addition, it provides a lot of growth to each employee as they have to teach each other their roles, skills, and responsibilities. An example was when I had a software release engineer and a project manager cross trained. By teaching each other, the engineer learned and grew some leadership, communication, and documentation skills. They practiced their technical skills further as they were very in tune with the technical training. They even made process improvements based on suggestions from the project manager. Ultimately, when the engineer resigned one day, the project manager was granted an opportunity to get hired. Role rotation has proved to be very popular over the years and has provided amazing results in my teams. And in the end, despite initial hesitation, everyone loves it as it adds to their résumés and personal and professional growth.

Stepping out of Your Comfort Zone Beyond your Career

Your comfort zone doesn't just exist at work. Everyone has a personal life comfort zone as well. Just like in your career, this can hold you back if it becomes *too* comfortable. Personally, I start off some mornings by taking a cold shower or plunging into a cold bath to just experience stepping out of my comfort zone. It might sound funny, odd, or perhaps just too cold to some, but when was the last time you did something with the purpose of stepping out of your comfort zone?

No one likes to be drenched in ice-cold water, but when you do this at 7 a.m., I assure you that you will be wide awake by 7:05 a.m. and will have lost the urge to get back into bed. Therefore, you are more productive by 7:30 a.m. than if you were just to wander sleepily throughout the first hour of your day.

Have you ever known anyone—or been someone—that stayed in a relationship because it was comfortable despite the fact that the relationship wasn't exactly what they (or you) wanted? On the flip side, some people become so comfortable on their own that they won't pursue a romantic relationship even though they have the desire to get married or have kids.

There are many reasons not to step out of your comfort zone but staying put can be counterproductive. Sometimes you have to be a little spontaneous and risky to make things happen!

I encourage the people I work with to try something new in their personal lives sometimes, especially if it is something they have doubts about. For example, I recently encouraged a team member to reach out to a volunteer organization and offer to help out. He was aligned with most of his goals but still felt a void. Although he found the idea of volunteering challenging, ultimately it met his need to make a difference in someone's life and he was glad he pushed himself to do it. It is important to remember that stepping out of your comfort zone is all about experiences, confidence, and personal growth.

PUTTING IT INTO PRACTICE

KEY TAKEAWAYS:

- Job descriptions are overrated. You will never know what an employer is really looking for, or what skills and personality traits they'll value, unless you go for it.
- When you get too comfortable, you stop looking for new opportunities.
- If the person before you could do the job, you are also capable of doing the job! Believe in yourself!

REFLECTION:

1. Delegate something that you are very comfortable doing to one of your employees while you mentor them, and then let go.
2. Think of something that you do very well at work (almost on autopilot). If you were to do a role rotation, what and from whom would you like to learn? Is this doable in your team?
3. Try out a new recipe.
4. Change up your workout routine.

Part Two

Short-Term Can Dos

CHAPTER 18

Time Management

My 20-plus years' experience in project management in the field of technology has greatly reduced my procrastination and boosted my track record of success. It has increased my focus and driven me to consistently deliver work on time. When all of these things flow together, my own stress and anxiety levels decrease and my productivity and efficiency increase.

If you work at an organization or a business where products or services are delivered or provided on a schedule, having a play-by-play plan helps enhance your performance and ensure that the goods and services are delivered and provided on time. Through effective strategies you are therefore able to achieve your goals with less effort.

What I have done that most people can't, won't, or don't do is maximize my time management skills to take me to the highest productivity level that I can achieve.

The more you practice time management skills, the more they become a part of your habits and daily routine. You'll find areas where you can overlap passive activities with active activities so that you can get more accomplished in less time. An active activity is when you give a task your entire concentration from start to finish, whereas a passive activity is where you start something and don't have to give it your full attention until the activity completes or hits a certain milestone. Over time, as you become more adept at this habit, you learn to more accurately estimate how long things take.

For example, if I need to boil water to make tea and also organize my day, I will automatically think of what I should start first to be most efficient. If I performed these tasks in serial order, taking 10 minutes to boil the water and then a further 10 minutes to organize my day, I would spend 20 minutes completing these actions. I've seen my friends and family do this sort of thing countless times.

I know to start heating the tea water first, and while it is heating, I'll sit down and focus on organizing my day—both things happen concurrently. In the end, I've spent around 12 minutes completing both tasks, saving at least eight minutes of my busy morning. I use this as an example we can easily visualize, however these are things we can implement at work as well. Think of areas in your work setting where you perhaps have to do something (active activity) and then wait for others to review, approve, or finish their tasks (this becomes your passive activity as you are waiting) in order for you to then continue. What tasks could you accomplish in this "dead time" while you wait?

When you look at things this way, time management becomes a balancing act. You have to learn how to balance the passive and active tasks to get more done in a shorter amount of time.

"Just like balancing active and passive activities, you want to balance your passions and your work life."

There is more to time management than just balancing tasks and maximizing the amount of stuff you get done in the shortest amount of time. One of the ways I have learned to manage my time more efficiently is in having a structured and integrated calendar for both my personal life and my work life in which I look ahead a day, a week, and sometimes more.

A Date and Time for Everything

Your time management calendar should be an hour-by-hour breakdown of what your day looks like—this is one level deeper than making plans and setting goals for yourself that we looked at in Chapter 2.

My work calendar has time sectioned off for everything. I have blocks of time to return phone calls, to check messages from Slack or Teams, email, and respond to them, and times blocked off for meetings. I block off an exact time for when a project is due and when milestones and all deadlines are to be met. It might seem a little obsessive to have such a structured calendar, but there are several benefits to following this style of time management plan.

First, you always know what is expected or due and what you should be doing at any given time. This eliminates uncertainty and keeps you focused on your tasks. While I write down my plan each morning, I visualize each activity as I do it throughout the day. This helps in minimizing distractions and helps me avoid procrastination.

> "The more you practice time management skills, the more they become a part of your habits and daily routine."

You'll never miss a deadline or fail to meet a client's expectations because you'll have it right on your calendar. Scheduling your deadlines also means you'll have to block off work time to make sure you complete everything before it is due, but knowing you've blocked the time will alleviate any stress or anxiety over your approaching deadline.

Another benefit is that you'll never miss any callbacks or emails that need to be answered, since you make the time to focus on those tasks instead of reactively answering emails all day long and then not having the right focus to get the main projects done.

Additionally, there will probably be days when you have too many meetings or work obligations, so it feels like you don't actually have time to do the work. When this happens, having a blocked-off schedule is so important because you'll be able to squeeze in as much work as possible between meetings, even if you have to overlap with your lunch break so you don't end up taking too much work home with you. This is particularly important nowadays when many people work remotely—you do not want to start cutting into your personal time by working into the evening after all the meetings are over.

I encourage my team to block off their schedule for planning and for getting the actual work done as far in advance as they can based on their project plans. This way, you can look ahead and make sure your days aren't crammed full of work meetings by letting people know when you are available—when you have no time blocked off in your calendar—versus when you aren't.

As I have expressed before, meeting our professional and personal goals are key to a balanced life and feeling happy, so I make sure I add a block of time to my calendar for my daily walks, my meditation, and my gym sessions. Also, it is important to be diligent and consistent at keeping to the times that you set as far as is possible. If someone wants to set a meeting for a particular time and day, but you have time blocked off to go to the gym or to answer emails, work with them to pick a different time when you don't already have a block in your schedule. Or if their matter cannot wait until the following day, you may need to be flexible and rearrange your schedule. However, your planning time and gym time should not always be the things that get rescheduled to meet other priorities, or you lose balance and do not achieve your goals.

Keeping that commitment of following your schedule every day will help you instill these time management skills into your daily routine. It maximizes efficiency and reduces stress. Sometimes it might not feel like it, but you do have control over your time and your schedule. That is why it is important to keep your time commitments.

At work, you probably have a scheduling tool like Outlook or Google Calendar to help manage your obligations. As a team leader, you should keep your calendar up to date and ensure nobody in your team sets their meetings over other meetings but instead looks for your availability if they need you. This sounds like common sense but is easier said than done—sometimes when you work in a large organization, there are usually more meetings than one can handle.

So, that is where your delegation skills come into play (more on delegation in Chapter 20). If you have a busy day coming up, don't hesitate to delegate to someone who can represent you in some of the meetings. Doing this frees up time for you to finish a few tasks at the top of your priority list. Be sure to block out some time for catching up with those people you delegated meetings to.

You could also have a team calendar that everyone on your team can see and access, so they can include team and project work obligations and avoid diary clashes. You might even want to have the option for them to add their own time blocks in the shared calendar for times when they have personal appointments that they won't be in the office for or personal time off for vacations.

It is also a good idea to work with your team on overlapping passive and active activities. You can do this by leading through example. My kids always call me the Queen of Multitasking because I overlap my passive and active activities, like planning my day while boiling water for my morning tea. Check in with your team from time to time. If you see them just waiting around for something to get finished, gently encourage them to find another small task they can work on while waiting for the initial task to be completed.

I schedule times for everything! If you look at my calendar, you'll see that I block off two lots of 30 minutes a day for "Planning time." This is the time I designate to go over my plans, goals, and schedules. I do this every day to ensure that I eliminate as much uncertainty, stress, and anxiety as possible. I put one block early in the morning for my personal planning time to help me meet my personal goals and the second during my working hours to ensure my team and I keep on top of our work plans and goals.

When you stick to your schedule, you keep yourself accountable and show yourself and others that you are reliable. You want to be the person that other people recognize as doing the things you say you'll do when you say you'll do them. I observe my friends and colleagues doing what they said they will do; however, they don't always do it at the time or on the day they said they would, which means I can only assume their clients and friends consider them to be somewhat reliable.

Scheduling "Down Time"

As part of your planning, you must also set aside time for your happiness and wellbeing—in other words, you need to schedule your own downtime. What is important to you? Is it going to the gym, going for a motorcycle ride, getting a massage, a meditation break, gardening, painting, walking, reading, sitting quietly and breathing for five minutes?

Making time for our passions, hobbies, and recharging our energy is vital. When you have a concrete, well-planned schedule, you'll be able to make time for these activities too. Sometimes, it can feel easy to rearrange your personal schedule in favor of your work life. You might think it is more important to put your work and work goals first. In some cases, that can be true, but personal care and passions shouldn't be ignored if you want to achieve sustainable and long-term career success.

Just like balancing active and passive activities, you want to balance your passions and your work life. This is one of the biggest paths to success and happiness that a lot of people can't, won't, or don't adhere to.

In your personal life, you can also work toward balancing multiple tasks, especially when it comes to chores, so that you can complete them faster and have more downtime. Something that has worked for me as good practice is to overlap common or related activities or activities that take place in the same physical space or area of the house. For example, if you are running the dishwasher or washing machine, sweep or vacuum until the load is done rather than going to the couch to sit and read while waiting.

That way, you'll have more uninterrupted downtime once your chores are out of the way, and you don't have to switch back and forth as much from enjoyable tasks to chores. Same as if, for example, I am going to the drycleaner's, I would have my list of what I need to pick up at the grocery store or pharmacy. I would wash the car, get gas, and run any other errands that may be in the same area, so I do not have to interrupt any of my other plans for the rest of the week.

Of course, in today's digital world, I am able to maximize my personal time by doing a lot of these errands online and getting things delivered, which frees up my personal time for things that are more productive, to expand my billable time—if I am charging for services—or simply to do things that are worth more to me personally. Achieving this balance requires accepting change in our lives, modifying our way of thinking, our routines, and building new habits. I have a close friend that always brings up how amazed he is by the number of things I get done in a day.

However, even though I have shared simple suggestions with him, such as depositing your checks digitally to save time instead of having to drive to the physical bank every week, believe it or not he still drives to the bank weekly. Rely on your bottled water delivery service, on your prepared meal service, or dog walkers, etc. I know it sounds way more expensive but when your work involves billing for your services hourly, it's easy to quantify the extra hours you have in your life in which to make more money. It's not about the hours you put in, it's about getting things done. Being results-oriented and disciplined in your time management applies both at home and whether you are working for a large or small organization.

You'll see in Chapters 19 and 20 how automation and delegation doesn't just help with time management and freeing up time but also helps you work toward success and happiness.

The more you practice this in your personal and work life, the more you'll find the best ways to maximize efficiency and make the most out of every minute of every day.

Being Spontaneous

As important as it is to stick to your schedule and be consistent with delivering what you say you will, when you say you will, sometimes life happens. It is okay to still be spontaneous, because every now and then you'll get a great opportunity you won't want to pass up! So, when a friend asks you to meet for dinner, do not immediately pass on the offer because it is not in your calendar. Be spontaneous, and if you want to go, then do it! The fact you have everything planned out allows you to easily get back to what you need to do or get done later.

Having a structured schedule doesn't eliminate flexibility. It eliminates stress, worry, procrastination and anxiety. It means that you'll never have to wonder what you should be doing with your time, and you'll be prepared to reschedule anything that needs to be rescheduled when something unexpected turns up.

Additionally, every now and then things on your schedule might need to be rearranged. If that happens, I'd recommend moving that scheduled item to a time slot within 24 hours. If you put it off too long, it could interfere with your project or clients' deadlines, or you might just keep putting it off and never getting it done.

So, remember, as important as your schedule and time commitments are, don't limit yourself to never being spontaneous or flexible. Otherwise, you could miss out on some great career and personal life events and opportunities.

As career driven as I have been all my life, I have also mastered the art of being spontaneous with my kids so that they can enjoy the wonders this life has to offer. My job is not only about being a high performer day in and day out, it is also to be the best mother

I can be. One way I have accomplished this is by taking my kids on spontaneous trips and making on-the-spot decisions that usually become our best memories.

One time, I was sent to work in Berlin, Germany, so I told my daughter I was flying her out there for a week to meet me there. We would spend a week learning about German history, trying new foods, and experiencing their customs and traditions. However, after three days we had done everything we wanted to do in Berlin and found ourselves at a train station looking at the schedule of trains departing in the next 20 minutes. We looked at each other like we were ready to go on an adventure, agreed that we would get on the next train that was departing, and ended up going to Poland for the day! I can't tell you how amazing this experience was. Bringing spontaneity into your life increases serotonin, a hormone that regulates our mood and feelings of wellbeing and happiness. When we embrace spontaneity in our lives—or work out, or spend time in the sun, or see loved ones—we produce serotonin, and the more we produce, the richer our life experiences can be.

Another time, I was at Miami Airport with my friend Michael, waiting to get on a plane to a friend's wedding in Brazil, when we realized we had forgotten to get our visas. His first response was distress that we would miss our vacation. Instead of just going home I asked at check-in where the next flight was heading that did not require a visa. In a couple of hours, he was on board with my spontaneity, and we were on our way to Buenos Aires, Argentina. Being spontaneous and resourceful with our tickets and hotel arrangements allowed us to enjoy an amazing vacation and create great memories we still talk about to this day, even though, unfortunately, we missed the wedding of someone close to our hearts.

Between you and me, this was not the only time I have had this type of adventure...but I'll save those stories for my next book.

PUTTING IT INTO PRACTICE

KEY TAKEAWAYS:

- Schedule downtime to refresh and relax.
- Combining active and passive tasks provides a good balance in your work and personal life.
- The more you practice time management skills, the more they become part of your daily routine.
- Have a date and time for everything.
- Give yourself permission to be spontaneous.

REFLECTION:

Think about what scheduling tool you will use: regular wall calendar, Outlook, your cell phone calendar etc. For work, will you use the same calendar across your team and integrate everyone's tasks? At home, will you have a family calendar with your kids' and partner's activities integrated?

Personal calendar:
1. Think of the items you want to do in a day that are personal: walk the dog, jog, go to the gym, take the kids to school, read, meditate, etc.
2. Figure out when you can have a block of personal time: every morning when you get up? After you drop the kids at school? At lunch or in the evening?
3. Input your personal activities at the most approximate times when you want to achieve them.
4. Set an alert or notification for each one to keep you on track.
5. Set an alarm for each one of them that you think you may want to avoid because they are hard for you. You can even change the label of the alarm and write something that inspires you to get it done!

Professional calendar:
1. Besides the meetings you need for the day, think of the activities you need to do to have a successful day at work: read/answer emails, make phone calls, planning, do paperwork, etc.

2. Add the above activities to your calendar at the times of day you are the most productive.
3. Set notifications and potential alarms for them as needed.
4. Follow your calendar!

Give yourself undivided attention when building your calendar/s.

Give yourself a realistic estimate on how long each item takes.

Revisit your calendars weekly!

Tweak whatever is not working and improve your process so you do not quit on building your new habit!

Be kind, and praise yourself when you stick to the planned items on your calendar.

CHAPTER 19

Automate the Repetitive

As well as time management tools, there are other ways that you can free up time for yourself and your team. One of those options is in automating repetitive tasks.

What I do that a lot of people can't, won't, or don't do is look for ways to automate anything repetitive in my day. Not only does this free up some of my own time, but it also increases efficiency.

> *"Not only does automation save you and your team time, it also allows you to be more productive."*

I get 200-plus emails a day. Catching up on them would be a full-time job if I didn't resort to automation. Now, I have filters to compartmentalize my inbox. I can prioritize which emails are most urgent and need immediate attention versus the ones that can wait, and more importantly, spam and others that I don't even need to review.

In the workspace, you can automate a lot of tasks. There are many services that can filter non-work-related emails and automate the sending out of marketing emails, promotions, and even social media posts. Through these services, you, or someone on your team, might only need to check it once a week or once a month to make sure that everything is functioning as it is supposed to—and update anything that needs updating—rather than checking it every day and spending hours of time developing and sending emails and writing social media posts.

Today, a lot of repetitive tasks are delegated to the computer and online services. Fortunately, there are plenty of ways to automate through computer systems. These same tools can be used in your personal life as well. Tracking finances, for example, can be incredibly time consuming, especially if you have multiple accounts and multiple credit cards. With programs like QuickBooks or Truebill, you can link all your accounts and it automatically tracks your finances without you updating spreadsheets every time you make a purchase or pay a bill.

Not only does automation save you and your team time, it also allows you to be more productive. Anything that is done in the background through automation still contributes to your daily productivity, because it helps you reach your overall goals.

I recommend using automation tools in as many areas of your life as you can. This can free up time, increase productivity, and reduce stress. Sometimes the repetitive tasks can be the most overwhelming.

Repetitive tasks, especially if they are seemingly small, can become stressful when there are a lot of other—larger—demands of your time. Taking those extra five minutes to write the same email every day is just tedious!

In the Greek story, Sisyphus, a man punished by the gods is tasked with rolling a massive boulder to the top of a mountain. When he reaches the summit and sets the boulder down, it rolls back to the bottom, and he must begin the task all over again. Nobody wants to feel like that in their work or homelife.

Testers in an engineering setting might at times get tired of performing the same repetitive tasks. This mental fatigue can lead to a higher risk of errors, physical fatigue with fingers, muscles and joints getting stiff and achy, or repetitive stress syndrome. Hence why there are test automation tools and capabilities created to avoid human errors as well as improve certain jobs.

When you introduce automation, you can focus better on the less repetitive tasks. I am always looking for ways to automate tasks at work, for myself and for my team. I have introduced many of my teams throughout the years to automation services and encourage them to then use the tools and knowledge to automate repetitive tasks for themselves in both at work and at home.

Automation for Reliability

Another great benefit of automation is increasing reliability. When you automate emails, the text is usually written out once and edited, and the same body is used any time that kind of email has to be sent. This eliminates human error, such as spelling mistakes if someone is rushing.

I like to think that if you want to do something, do it once, do it right. Since repetitive tasks can be daunting, a lot of people like to rush through them, which leads to more potential for human error.

Whenever you or your team undertake a task, you are representing your company and yourselves. If human error becomes common, then it can reflect poorly on your professionalism.

Fortunately, the programs and services that help with automation, such as Calendly, Grammarly, and Xero are reliable. Whether you use them in your company or in your personal life, nowadays you can automate paying your bills, having your computer cleaned for viruses, schedule your robot vacuum, get your shopping on Amazon, or your groceries delivered regularly. You can free up time, increase productivity, and reduce human error. All of this contributes to success in your career, your team's success, and the extra time you free up to invest in other things.

It is, of course, true that there are plenty of tasks and activities in your work and personal life that can't be automated. That is why it is so important to automate whatever you can.

PUTTING IT INTO PRACTICE

KEY TAKEAWAYS:

- Automation saves you and your team time.
- Automation increases productivity.
- Automation leads to reliability and removes human error.

REFLECTION:

1. What are common tasks that come up regularly for you?
2. Do some research into what email filters may work for you.
3. Ask your team for their suggestions for automating some activities. They may come up with a few you haven't thought of.
4. In your personal life, are there any monthly payments that you can automate? Any monthly shopping that you can set up to be delivered?
5. Are there any scheduled services that you can automate monthly, biweekly, etc. so you do not have to go back to planning the schedule?

CHAPTER 20

Delegate So You Can Focus on Being Your Best

When I first moved into a leadership position, one of the hardest lessons I learned was how to delegate rather than do everything myself. Fortunately, I was able to ease into it by assessing my team members' strengths and weaknesses, clearly communicating my expectations, and establishing trust. The key was getting the right people to focus on the right tasks.

Moving from a position where you do everything yourself to delegating to teammates comes with a period of transition, a lot of trust, and the belief that the other person is capable. In a leadership role it is important to establish yourself as a delegator early on. If you don't, it will become habit to take on the majority of the work, which will lead to challenges with your career goals (if growing as a leader is still in your goals, which I will outline later in the chapter).

Many employees in search of career advancement or leadership positions can't, don't, or won't delegate tasks to others. This leads to them getting stuck in their roles. What helped me learn to delegate was thinking that delegation gives opportunities for growth to others, more specifically, the members of my team. I surround myself with people I can trust and rely on, then I can delegate tasks to them—and mentor them on how to assist me—and in return, I get more time to be able to take on more responsibility and grasp more opportunities.

Think of it this way: If you are always too busy doing the bulk of the work, then your calendar will always be booked, and you will be inaccessible to your bosses or to your team if they need your support. Inadvertently, this can cause you to miss out on some great advancement opportunities and could damage the relationship you have with your team. Although it is unintentional, when you don't delegate to your team, they can feel like you don't trust them enough to handle a task. So, what I realized was that by delegating I am giving my team the opportunity to grow individually and in their career paths as well with me.

Through delegation, I've been able to expand my leadership umbrella by extending my presence through the actions of others. It is a way to fully engage team members and opens up options like hiring consultants or freelancers that will contribute their best and specialized work to our shared priorities. It has also been a great way to get to know and work with so many wonderful individuals.

If you look at delegation as an act of offering opportunities to others, it can seem much less intimidating. Through delegation you can achieve more of your career goals long term. For example, by delegating, my bosses are more likely to notice me because delegation increases overall productivity and efficiency on my team and reflects positively on me and my leadership skills. Rather than one person trying to carry the whole load, our tasks can be spread throughout the whole team, and that means more weight can be pulled over a shorter distance or amount of time. As a result, I am recognized as a stronger, more effective leader. These traits continue to open up opportunities for me in my career, and they can do the same for you too!

Delegate What You Don't Have to Do

I am always delegating tasks to my team that I am not required to do myself. You may think you can do all, but teams are built for a reason and working together and finishing projects becomes faster and more fun as a team, knowing you are fulfilling a company's vision. You should never think that you have to do it all on your own. You have a great team of employees to help you get things done!

Sometimes, you might need to mentor an individual team member, or the whole team, on a particular task, but not only does that expand their knowledge base, it gives you the chance to work directly with them and create a bond of trust. More than that, once they know what is expected, you can delegate that task whenever you need to.

There may be some tasks or project elements that your company or team are not equipped to handle. When this happens, it can be beneficial to learn a new skill, but this can be very time consuming unless you are able to schedule it in and know it will serve you well in the future. This is where freelancers and consultants come in.

A lot of companies will hire freelancers, contractors, or consultants for the duration of a project to bring in expertise and skills that they otherwise aren't capable of at the time. This is another form of delegation and can be immensely stress-relieving to both you and your team.

Hiring a subject matter expert as a temporary contractor for the duration of a project takes a lot of the pressure off you and your team to work too far outside of your skillset without having to learn an entirely new one. While I always encourage people to develop their knowledge and learn new skills, sometimes that isn't realistic for certain tasks.

For example, drawing blueprints is an architectural skill that requires going to school and getting a degree. If your company or team doesn't have any architects on staff, and a project needs blueprints, outsourcing or contracting is the best option to get the work done to the highest standards without sacrificing your own time or the quality of work.

While being a team leader means that you have the power of delegation, you want to encourage your team members to develop this skill as well. Without turning your team members against each other, you can always extend a small amount of power to individuals that have a certain knowledge or skillset, giving them the leeway to help delegate tasks that relate specifically to their skillset or knowledge.

Not only does spreading the responsibility take more pressure off you and free up more of your time to accomplish other tasks, it lets your team members exercise their strengths and work on their own delegation skills. This prepares them to step into higher leadership roles when the opportunity arises and helps set them up for success.

Freeing Up Your Personal Time

In my personal life, I delegate everything I can, as well. I see my friends spending a lot of their time on tasks like cooking, mowing the lawn, walking their dogs, etc. They say that they love these things and then they wonder why their time management is not so great. These are time-consuming activities that can take away from the time and energy that could be applied to personal hobbies and passions. If you love cooking, mowing your lawn, and walking your dog then go ahead and enjoy them, but my point is, where possible, choose the things that you don't like doing and delegate them to someone else.

In my personal life, I prefer to hire people to perform some of the daily tasks that I don't *have* to do myself. While this can get expensive, it frees up so much of my time and I also avoid getting burnout, as I have learned there are no points to be won for doing everything myself. You can make up for the financial part by advancing your career more quickly with more time to focus on it.

Where you live there may be neighborhood kids that always want to make a few extra bucks by lawn mowing and dog walking. By letting them do your chores, not only do you free your own time up, but they get some pocket money. By paying for other services, you provide business opportunities and financial stability to other people whose livelihoods depend on paying clients. This is another mutually beneficial form of delegation.

PUTTING IT INTO PRACTICE

KEY TAKEAWAYS:

- Delegate what you don't have to do yourself.
- Free up your time through delegation—keep regular business hours and don't use up all your free time on mundane chores.
- Trust your team to carry out tasks—don't carry all the responsibility yourself.

REFLECTION:

1. Write a list of recurrent things you usually do or feel you have to do, for example paying the bills, mowing the lawn, gardening, walking the dog, etc.
2. Think about the people in your life that are part of your team (partner, kids, neighbors).
3. What items from your list can you assign and to whom? And which items can you hire people to do for you?
4. Think about trade-offs—rather than mowing the lawn, wouldn't it be better to spend time on launching your own business? There are a lot of easy to use, not overly expensive services for things like lawn mowing, gardening, dog walking, etc. You don't have to break the bank to delegate these tasks.
5. Now, do the same for your office work. What are the things you currently do that can be delegated to someone in your team?
6. What things are you not comfortable delegating and why?
7. Why don't you trust your team members to do a particular task? What can go wrong? How can you train them? How can you develop trust in this area?

CHAPTER 21

Celebrate Your Team and Your Life Often

You never want your job to feel like a boring nine-to-five position where the only thing that matters is the bottom line. This is a sure-fire way to feel stuck or feel like you are never advancing and never feeling happy or fulfilled in your career.

It is common for people to feel stuck and unhappy in their jobs. I often hear friends and family complain about their jobs. Maybe you do too? In Chapter 10, we talked about being passionate and finding something to be passionate about even if you aren't exactly where you want to be.

That passion is so important for happiness and success. One way to help you establish that passion is by celebrating your team, your life, and your victories—big and small.

What I do that a lot of managers and leaders can't, won't, or don't do is celebrate with my team and celebrate my own life. I regularly go for happy hour celebration drinks with my team to ensure that we all remember what it is like to have pleasurable moments in life and appreciate the goals and accomplishments we've achieved. Often, these gatherings come after a win of some kind, so we can all share in the positive energy of that great accomplishment.

Not only do we all enjoy the achievement together and relax after the hard work of meeting that goal, but it refreshes us and inspires us to put the same hard work into the next goal or project.

As a team, we are all working toward a common goal. When we have these group celebrations, we become a singular unit enjoying a common victory rather than feeling like individuals all working toward something different. It also provides opportunities outside the office or work environment to meet as social beings and to develop a relationship and have conversations we would not have in the office or when working virtually.

I also like to celebrate both big and small victories in my personal life. Whether this celebration consists of drinks with family, going out with friends, or treating myself to something special, I make sure to remind myself what the celebration/acknowledgment is for. This helps me to see my progress in my personal goals and gives me something to look forward to each time I accomplish something.

> *"When you build healthy, supportive relationships like these, you are also showing a reflection of how you feel about yourself."*

A close friend of mine often jokes about how he thinks I'm always partying or celebrating something, even when I am simply hanging out with my kids. I think this goes to show how I feel about celebrating and enjoying life after working hard. You should encourage your team to celebrate their personal wins and achievements—big and small—too. When your team members tell you about something in their personal lives that they accomplished, offer praise and compliments. Even if they don't think it is a big deal, offer them a celebratory sentiment so they see the value in it.

More than that, celebration increases confidence, whether that is career or personal life related. This is why I say it is important to celebrate both the big and the little wins, because it all contributes to confidence, pleasure, and happiness.

Your Team Is Your Family

By engaging in group activities with your team, especially celebrations, you help establish a family dynamic within that team, with a certain comradery that encourages everyone concerned to work together, create a bond, and strive for more.

During the working week, you probably spend most of your waking time with your team. They become your work family, in a sense. Now, all families have their moments of friction, and the best way to reduce that is to have fun together and blow off steam.

Again, this is where my concept of happy hour celebrations comes into play. At these gatherings, your team members have the chance to build relationships outside of the workplace. It fosters a more positive work environment, reminds everyone that your work is a team effort, and it can be a good time to reflect on everyone's contributions and how that led to the team's success.

I personally am so proud of my current team. We have all put in the work to grow our relationships with each other to the point where everyone truly feels like family. I'm sure if you do the same, your work life will be less of a drag and more exciting.

Celebrate the Big and Little Accomplishments

I've always believed that it is important to celebrate the little wins as much as the big ones. Big wins happen less often, so it is an important reminder that you are working toward something bigger when you celebrate smaller achievements.

This helps you see the progress you're making toward your goals, reminds you what you're working toward, and helps to relieve intermittent stress and frustration that can accumulate between the big wins.

I like to celebrate my big and little achievements in both my work and in my personal life. A big work achievement could be finishing a project on time. Little work achievements could be creating a project outline or hitting progress milestones throughout.

A big win in your personal life could be getting that house or condo you wanted. A little win could be something like successfully baking your first batch of cookies or achieving your step goal every day for a week.

As I said before, celebrating the big and little wins helps to build confidence. It inspires you and your team to know you are on target and energizes you to do more, work harder, and set higher expectations for yourself—raising the bar, as we discussed in Chapter 7.

Surround Yourself with People That Inspire You and Make You Better

I believe that a fundamental part of celebrating my life and my team is surrounding myself with people that inspire me, allow me to grow, and make me better. I always build my teams with people that have strengths in areas where I might lack them, who I see great potential in, and who have interesting and unique skills to offer. These traits are inspiring to me and to my other team members. It can also create a healthy amount of competition for my team members to work harder and be better by knowing that everyone is competent in the team, and nobody gets left behind.

I surround myself with friends in a social circle of people that are smarter than me, energetic, ambitious, and passionate—people that encourage me to be the best me I can be. I seek out relationships with people that inspire me to do new things or with people that encourage me to come up with new and innovative ideas.

I encourage the people I mentor or coach to also surround themselves with such inspiring, encouraging people. You may have heard the phrase: The people you surround yourself with is who you become. I always taught my kids to be selective about whom they socialize with. Why? Because whether you want to believe this or not, your environment affects you more than you know. If you surround yourself with people who lack ambition, are lazy, and are always negative, it will either be draining or will rub off on you. However, when you surround yourself with people who are hungry, driven, money-motivated, have great values, are always positive, and are kind to others, those traits will also rub off on you.

It can be hard to see our own victories or stick to our own goals without having supportive people in our lives. That is why I say surrounding yourself with these kinds of people plays such an important part in celebrating your life. When you build healthy, supportive relationships like these, you are also showing a reflection of how you feel about yourself.

When confident, happy people surround themselves with friends, family, and a social circle that have the same mindset as them, success and personal growth will follow. Your social circle, in and out of work, is a reflection of your goals, happiness, and successes. It comes down to what you think you deserve and what you think you are worth.

Know your worth and show it by celebrating your life and by filling it with people that are inspiring and make you want to be better.

PUTTING IT INTO PRACTICE

KEY TAKEAWAYS:

- Your team is like your family—celebrate them often and encourage social activities outside of the office.
- When you build healthy, supportive relationships, you are also showing a reflection of how you feel about yourself.
- Surround yourself with people that inspire you to make yourself better.
- Celebrate big and little accomplishments—celebrate your life often.

REFLECTION:

1. Think of things you are trying to accomplish personally and professionally. What is the next "small" step or accomplishment that, once you make it, will make you feel happy and want to celebrate?
2. What things are your kids, your spouse, or partner accomplishing that deserve to be celebrated?
3. What milestones have your team reached that should be celebrated?
4. Set up a happy hour "just because" and invite your whole team.

CHAPTER 22

Building Teams

One of the keys to my success is that I know how to build the best team to work with me. As a leader, I know that my team is a reflection on me. Their success is linked to my success, and if I don't have the support of an A-team, then I won't be able to reach my career goals. So, I've come up with a solid formula for how to staff the best team possible!

How to Build the Best Team

In some workplaces, the concept of team-building gets a bad reputation—some leaders even dread this aspect of their jobs. They see team-building as an uncomfortable activity and a clichéd icebreaker. What I do that other leaders can't, won't, or don't do is bypass this awkwardness by building teams without letting them know they are being built. I must admit, this took me years of experience with building many, many teams.

As a consultant, and even as an employee, I would always get assigned the challenging projects that for some reason others had failed at delivering before me. Besides focusing on the project needs, of course, my main focus has always been on building the right team either to save that failing project or simply to work with me from beginning to end or to support a particular function. That team is your support mechanism and becomes part of your daily life.

I learned that through building trust, mitigating conflict, encouraging communication and respect, and increasing collaboration that I can create the foundation for how the whole team should interact. I identify the strengths and weaknesses of those on my team, their work styles, and personal needs, as we all have different needs in life. I know how to put together a high-performance team, resulting in more engaged employees or contractors, higher morale, less drama, and a group of people who are eager, have ambition, and strive for success. When you put it all together, this is a first-class, loyal, resilient, and productive team.

Over the years, many people have sought my assistance on interacting successfully with teams. Here are my tips:

- I am willing to invest in my team and to train them in what is needed for the job.
- I select people who I know won't expect to be micromanaged and can work independently and without being watched over to deliver what is at hand as well as demonstrating they go above and beyond what is asked of them.
- I put my employees in positions to grow and learn.
- I actively ask for feedback on what is working and what isn't.
- I don't ask them to do anything I wouldn't do myself.
- I regularly rotate role responsibilities so everyone has an opportunity to learn and grow and showcase who may be the best fit for certain areas or jobs. This last point I learned by observing how many companies often only have one employee with knowledge in a particular area and when that person wants to take time off, it becomes such a challenge to cover their work.

There will be times when I look beyond the résumé of an applicant. It makes them more appreciative to have the job and the opportunity, which means they will want to work harder.

I've known former employees and contractors that leave their jobs and who, after having worked in other companies, come back—at the time of writing this book, my current company is a prime example. I believe this company is an amazing place to work. People who once left have mentioned how much they learned, grew, and felt part of an amazing team, so they came back. Not all team members are the same. I've also had employees quit working for me because the high-performance expectations were too much for them to handle, but after they work elsewhere for a while, most call me and ask to come work for me again. They feel that their new role lacked the professional growth aspect of becoming part of a high-performance team and being a high performer themselves.

By giving my team members the freedom to tackle challenges independently, they grow and feel like they are contributing to the team, department, and organization. If I always gave them the answers, they'd never feel like they were growing into their role or beyond their role to something new and better. They'd feel stuck and undervalued. I share this as I see so many other leaders sometimes afraid to delegate to their teams as they believe that they cannot come up with the solutions by themselves, which is not true. Allow them to grow with you.

I use the planning skills from Chapter 2 to create opportunities for everyone on my team. I work hard to build their trust in me, and in each other, allowing them to do more. By trusting their peers, they are able to answer their own questions, learn new skills, and become part of an overall more successful team. In his book, *All In: How Impactful Teams Build Trust from the Inside Out*, Robb Holman talks about how so much of effective leadership comes down to how you build trust with your team (Holman, 2019).

One of my employees once gave the feedback, "Everyone on the team is someone I know would have my back and cover for me if needed." This is a sentiment everyone on my team shares, trusting each other the same way they trust me.

Before I even get to the point of building my team, I first have to choose the right people to put on my team. Here is how I do it:

I hire:

- People that cover my weaknesses—yes, they need to be strong in areas where I am weak.
- People that are totally hungry to work and hungry for success.
- Energetic and positive people.
- People who are focused on the activities needed for the job and not just people who look good on paper.
- People who have chemistry with me and the rest of the team.
- People willing to cross train and rotate responsibilities, allowing for other team members to take time off and have a more balanced family/work/personal life.
- People who inspire trust and are trustworthy.
- People that are humble, even as they strive for success.
- Results-oriented people.
- Team-oriented people.
- People that have a sense of urgency with their work.
- People who are loyal, or who I think will become loyal.

Most of the time, I also ask other team members for their input on new hires so the whole team is involved. As we know, résumés can say anything we write on them, so I have come up with a universal interview question that tells me a lot about a person's qualities beyond what I can read on their résumé.

I ask, "How do you make an omelet?" Their response—the simplicity, complexity, planning steps, etc.—always gives me an idea about how they'll fit with my team, even if they can't cook or have never made an omelet. It shows how humble, flexible, or transparent the person is about their cooking skills and whether they have a sense of humor.

I have colleagues that ask about the books a prospective employee reads or what they do for fun. Whatever gives you that insight into their personality would work so you can have a simple conversation and get to know each other a little bit. After all, an interview usually only takes a couple of hours, but then you spend at least eight hours a day with that person when they are hired.

Find your own interview question that will provide insight into the qualities you look for in your team members. Remember, building a team with the right people is going to be a huge component to your success and happiness in your career. A lot of the interactions you have with your team—the dynamic you build with them—can also be applied to your relationships in your personal life with friends and family. You can learn a lot about interpersonal relationships by the way you work with your team.

PUTTING IT INTO PRACTICE

KEY TAKEAWAYS:

- Invest in building the best team possible for yourself and your projects.
- Recognize what skills are needed the most in your teams.
- Encourage trust between team members by getting them to work collaboratively with each other and to cross train them.

REFLECTION:

1. Who is in your team? How well do you know them?
2. I don't ask them to do anything I wouldn't do myself. Do you know how to do what your team does? If not, learn from them.
3. Have you thought about what drives each member of your team? What are their needs and wants?
4. Does your team have sense of urgency? Are your team members results-oriented? How are they measured for success? Do they know how they are evaluated and how they are doing?
5. Do your team members trust each other? Get them to read *The Speed of Trust: The One Thing That Changes Everything*, by Stephen M. R. Covey.
6. Do you need to replace some members? Are you building a new team from scratch?

CHAPTER 23

The Power of Taking Care of Your Body

Work on Your Physical Energy Consistently

The power of taking care of your body is as important as any other tip and trick I have talked about in this book. And even though we do not go in depth on all my tricks in this book, I do want to share some that I think are critical to being at your peak performance. You have to keep your physical and emotional energy in check to achieve your goals in both your career and personal life. If you're too burned out all the time, you'll get cranky, frustrated, and feel too tired to get things done. This is counterproductive to your personal success.

What a lot of people can't, won't, or don't do is take care of their bodies, to recharge their physical and emotional energies consistently throughout the day, keeping themselves focused and on their A-game.

I exercise and stretch daily. I start each morning by stretching before I take a look at my phone or do anything else. Even if, for some reason, my blocked time for the gym gets impacted, I work around that by taking the stairs instead of the elevator, parking my car in the furthest parking spot wherever I go to during the day to get my steps in, or doing a power walk at the end of the day. Those steps and ensuring that I incorporate physical movement into my day is a great way to rejuvenate my body and keep my energy up. I also ensure that every 50–60 minutes, I get up and walk to get water or stretch for a few seconds between meetings.

Another method of replenishing energy is through power naps. A quick 10-minute nap during a break or when you first get home from work is a great way to get your second wind and give yourself a boost of energy. Just like having a morning routine is important in setting up the day for success, having an evening routine that wraps up the day and allows time to prepare for the following day and mentally and physically winds you down is so powerful. Taking a bath, reading a book, or enjoying a (non-caffeinated) hot drink are some things to try.

Good nutrition, eating healthy, and feeding your mind and body properly are essential. Preparing meals in advance—even doing a whole week of prep for breakfasts, lunches, and dinners in one day if you can—reduces the time you need to spend thinking about food each day and helps you craft healthier meals than if you just went to open the refrigerator when you're hungry, trying to figure out what to eat or what to order.

Some other tips I use for restoring and maintaining daily energy levels include:

- Journaling or keeping a gratitude journal.
- Meditation.
- Having a daily planner with inspirational quotes.
- Exercising when feeling down and daily physical activity.
- Having my purpose written down and thinking about my "Why" daily so that I am on track.
- Asking myself, "What can I do for others today?"

You'll notice that my list includes a lot of the items talked about in previous chapters. This is a simpler breakdown of some of the tools or routines I use to keep myself at the top of my game so I can reach all levels of success in my career and in my personal life while feeling happy, having good relationships, feeling fulfilled, and staying balanced.

PUTTING IT INTO PRACTICE

KEY TAKEAWAYS:

- Have a routine for the morning and at bedtime.
- Keep a gratitude journal.
- Practice self-care daily.
- Exercise daily, especially when feeling down.
- Take time to plan meals and ensure good nutrition.

REFLECTION:

1. How is your physical energy? How do you restore and maintain your energy levels daily?
2. Remind yourself of your "Why." Write it down and think about your purpose.
3. Are you contributing to others? What can you do for others today?

CHAPTER 24

Final Thoughts

Everyone is capable of being successful and happy. Everyone has it within themselves to change their life for the better. Believe it or not, you CAN have it all—you can make your dreams of success and happiness a reality, you can find balance, and you can live your life with passion, both in your career and in your personal life.

We have covered a lot of ground and I believe that with what I have shared in this book you will have a stronger understanding of the simple skills, habits, and strategies that, if applied consistently, can truly help you change your life. The best advice that I can give you is this: First, define what success means to you. Then apply what you have learned here and go get it! Go and achieve your goals!

By being open to doing what others can't, won't, or don't do, I have given myself many opportunities that I am so grateful for. At times I was afraid or hesitant about taking action because I didn't want to be different. I worried about what others would say or think about me always trying to be the best version of myself. But I learned to not care about what others said, to keep pushing, and to never take "No" for an answer. I learned I could do what others can't, won't, or don't do and got to create the ideal work–life balance for myself.

It took me time, multiple painful experiences, and a lot of hard lessons to get to where I am today. I worked hard to establish myself professionally and to find balance. Attaining success and happiness hasn't always been easy as a woman in the corporate world, as a single mom, or as someone who wasn't born in the US. I overcame those obstacles and proved a lot of people wrong, including myself at times! What I offer to you in this book is a short cut. By utilizing my experience and the tools and tricks I've relied on every day, you can leap ahead, defy the status quo, and accelerate your own learning curve.

The details in this book are your starting point to begin making changes in your routines and thought patterns that will benefit your success and happiness overall. Now that I've whet your appetite, there is so much more I can teach you, layers upon layers to dig through that will ensure you follow in the footsteps of other successful people I've mentored.

When I started mentoring and coaching others, I worked with some young, recent college graduates who, through following my advice and guidance, advanced through their careers and reached staggering six-figure salaries in a fraction of the time that other people of their age and career demographic usually manage to do. You can do that too, regardless of your age or where you are in your career today.

By slipping into the role of doing what others can't, won't, or don't do, and by utilizing the skills in this book, you'll outshine other professionals around you.

Cici Gets Shit Done

Over the years, many of my peers and coworkers have often told me that I "get shit done." It's true. I push myself ahead and I work hard to achieve what needs doing. I go above and beyond in my career and in my personal life to get what I want so I can live the way I choose to live.

If, after reading this book, my ideas and concepts resonate with you and motivate you to have a life filled with passion, excitement, and energy, then I wholeheartedly invite you to reach out to me so I can help you on the path to achieving those goals. I know from personal experience that making changes isn't always easy! If you are struggling with any of these concepts, time spent with a life coach or counselor who can guide you with planning, organization, and clarity in your life might just be the key you need to unlock your mindset and do what others can't, won't, or don't do to get ahead of the game and reach success and happiness faster!

Connect with Me:

Instagram: @Cici_Castelli

https://www.cicicastelli.com

https://www.linkedin.com/in/cicicastelli/

https://www.facebook.com/CiciCastelli

ACKNOWLEDGMENTS

I hope you have enjoyed reading my stories, because they helped me get to where I am today. This book would never have been possible without a few of the people in my life.

My mamá—for my strong foundation, teaching me ethics and values, guiding me on how to raise my kids, and most importantly, for role modeling resiliency and never giving up, even when things get tough in life, which has allowed me to become who I am today.

My children—for inspiring me to be a better version of myself every day, believing in me as a contributor to society, always giving me opportunities to influence you and your friends, supporting me during this adventure and journey of self-discovery, and for sharing your friendship so generously!

My daughter Bianca—for helping me tons with the editing and reminding me of so many examples to use in this book.

My son Giancarlo—for helping me with the creation of the book with your altruism, generous time, and candid feedback.

I would like to thank every leader I have worked for and with for believing in me and my strategies and for the many opportunities given and lessons learned.

Also, thank you to my current team for their support, trust, and the opportunity to be their leader.

Finally, I would like to acknowledge my great partner, friend, and attorney Ian M. Berkowitz for encouraging me to write this book and supporting me immensely throughout.

REFERENCES

Briggs, B. (2018). "White Flag." from *Church of Scars*. 3 mins, 51 secs.

Burey, J. and Tulshyan, R. (2021). "Stop Telling Women They Have Imposter Syndrome." *Harvard Business Review*. https://hbr. org/2021/02/stop-telling-women-they-have-imposter-syndrome.

Covey, S. R. (2020). *The 7 Habits on the Go: Timeless Wisdom for a Rapidly Changing World*. (Miami, FL: Mango Media).

Covey, S. M. R. (2008). *The Speed of Trust: The One Thing That Changes Everything*. New York, NY: Free Press).

Covey, S. R. (1989). *The 7 Habits of Highly Effective People*. (New York, NY: Free Press).

Franklin Institute, The. (n.d.). "Edison's Lightbulb." https://www. fi.edu/history-resources/edisons-lightbulb.

Gandhi, M. K. and Desai, M. H., trans. (1993). *Gandhi an Autobiography: The Story of My Experiments with Truth*. (Boston, MA: Beacon Press).

Grant, A. (2021). *Think Again: The Power of Knowing What You Don't Know*. (New York, NY: Viking).

Graziosi, D. (2019). *Millionaire Success Habits: The Gateway to Wealth & Prosperity*. (Carlsbad, CA: Hay House Business).

Harari, O. (2002). *The Leadership Secrets of Colin Powell*. (New York, NY: McGraw Hill Education).

Hessekiel, D. (2021). "The Rise and Fall of the Buy-One-Give-One Model at TOMS." Forbes. https://www.forbes.com/sites/davidhessekiel/2021/04/28/the-rise-and-fall-of-the-buy-one-give-one-model-at-toms/?sh=2fe045ab71c4.

Hewlett, S. A. (2014). *Executive Presence: The Missing Link Between Merit and Success*. (New York, NY: Harper Business).

History.com Editors. (2019). "Hellen Keller." History.com. https://www.history.com/topics/womens-rights/helen-keller.

Holman, R. (2019). *All In: How Impactful Teams Build Trust from the Inside Out*. (Morrisville, NC: Lulu Publishing Services).

Keller, H. (1903). *The Story of My Life; Helen Keller's Autobiography*. (New York, NY: Doubleday, Page & Co.).

Lavanya, N. and Malarvizhi, T. (2008). "Risk analysis and management: a vital key to effective project management." Project Management Institute. https://www.pmi.org/learning/library/risk-analysis-project-management-7070.

McKeown, G. (2014). *Essentialism: The Disciplined Pursuit of Less*. (New York, NY: Currency).

Morrissey, M. (2017). "The Power of Writing Down Your Goals and Dreams." *Huffpost*. https://www.huffpost.com/entry/the-power-of-writing-down_b_12002348.

Sanborn, M. (2006). *You Don't Need a Title to Be a Leader: How Anyone, Anywhere, Can Make a Positive Difference*. (New York, NY: Currency).

Selk, Jason. (2013). "Habit Formation: The 21-Day Myth." *Forbes*. https://www.forbes.com/sites/jasonselk/2013/04/15/habit-formation-the-21-day-myth/?sh=7f9e484ddebc.

Shneider, M. (2018). "How Google Built a Culture That Inspires New Ideas Every Day." *Inc*. https://www.inc.com/michael-schneider/how-google-built-a-culture-that-inspires-new-ideas-every-day.html.

Schwantes, M. (2017). "Steve Jobs Once Gave Some Brilliant Management Advice on Hiring Top People." *Inc*. https://www.inc.com/marcel-schwantes/this-classic-quote-from-steve-jobs-about-hiring-employees-describes-what-great-leadership-looks-like.html.

Tracy, B. (n.d.). "How to Create an Action Plan." Brian Tracy International. https://www.briantracy.com/blog/personal-success/how-to-create-an-action-plan/.

Tracy, B. (2012). *The Power of Self-Confidence: Become Unstoppable, Irresistible, and Unafraid in Every Area of Your Life.* (Hoboken, NJ: Wiley).

Lightning Source UK Ltd.
Milton Keynes UK
UKHW021017060522
402558UK00010B/2104

9 798985 560305